D1293660

HowExpert Guide to Phlebotomy

70 Tips to Learning about Blood Draws, Lab Work, Panels, Plasma, Tests, and the Profession of a Phlebotomist

HowExpert with MacKenna Balsewicz

Copyright HowExpert™
www.HowExpert.com

For more tips related to this topic, visit HowExpert.com/phlebotomy.

Recommended Resources

- HowExpert.com –How To Guides by Everyday Experts.
- HowExpert.com/free – Free HowExpert Email Newsletter.
- HowExpert.com/books – HowExpert Books
- HowExpert.com/courses – HowExpert Courses
- HowExpert.com/clothing – HowExpert Clothing
- HowExpert.com/membership – HowExpert Membership Site
- HowExpert.com/affiliates – HowExpert Affiliate Program
- HowExpert.com/jobs – HowExpert Jobs
- HowExpert.com/writers – Write About Your #1 Passion/Knowledge/Expertise & Become a HowExpert Author.
- HowExpert.com/resources – Additional HowExpert Recommended Resources
- YouTube.com/HowExpert – Subscribe to HowExpert YouTube.
- Instagram.com/HowExpert – Follow HowExpert on Instagram.
- Facebook.com/HowExpert – Follow HowExpert on Facebook.
- TikTok.com/@HowExpert – Follow HowExpert on TikTok.

Publisher's Foreword

Dear HowExpert Reader,

HowExpert publishes quick 'how to' guides on all topics from A to Z by everyday experts.

At HowExpert, our mission is to discover, empower, and maximize everyday people's talents to ultimately make a positive impact in the world for all topics from A to Z...one everyday expert at a time!

All of our HowExpert guides are written by everyday people just like you and me, who have a passion, knowledge, and expertise for a specific topic.

We take great pride in selecting everyday experts who have a passion, real-life experience in a topic, and excellent writing skills to teach you about the topic you are also passionate about and eager to learn.

We hope you get a lot of value from our HowExpert guides, and it can make a positive impact on your life in some way. All of our readers, including you, help us continue living our mission of positively impacting the world for all spheres of influences from A to Z.

If you enjoyed one of our HowExpert guides, then please take a moment to send us your feedback from wherever you got this book.

Thank you, and we wish you all the best in all aspects of life.

Sincerely,

BJ Min
Founder & Publisher of HowExpert
HowExpert.com

PS...If you are also interested in becoming a HowExpert author, then please visit our website at HowExpert.com/writers. Thank you & again, all the best!

Table of Contents

Chapter 1: Learning the Basics of Phlebotomy

Key terms in this chapter: Vein, Artery, Blood, Instruments, Patients.

Simple Steps of a Lab Draw

Tip #1: Patient Identifiers

The most important part of phlebotomy is making sure you have the correct patient. Each patient must be identified with two patient identifiers: their name and their birthday. For every patient I have, I begin by saying, "Hello! My name is Mackenna, and I will be your phlebotomist today! Can I get your first name, last name, and birth date, please?" This is the most effective because it provides the beginning of a dialogue between us. There have been times when I have walked into the wrong patient room, and doing this necessary step, saved me from sticking the wrong patient. When working at a clinic, I call my patients back by their first name, which is why I need to verify the last name and birth date so the wrong patient doesn't come back. You must also scan the patient's wristband in the hospital to confirm that you have the correct patient. Scanning the wrist band will bring up all of the active orders for that patient that need to be drawn. When labeling a tube, I hold the cap in my left hand and write from left to right–my initials, the date (mm/dd/yyyy), and the time in 24-hour format (0000-2400). Below this, I write the patient's last name, a comma, and their first name. Below that, I write their birthdate in the same (mm/dd/yyyy) format as the date.

Tip #2: Arm Positioning

When you get a feel for the profession of phlebotomy, you will find the position that is the most comfortable for you to draw patients in. There is a magic to positioning the arm of a patient and the way it changes the appearance of the vein. Right now, look down at the crook of your elbow where your antecubital vein is located. For some people who have very prevalent veins, you will be able to see them. Do they stand out more when your arm is completely straight with your palm up or when your elbow is bent slightly? For those of you who can't see your veins, they are more prevalent when the arm is extended and flexed forward with the palm up. If you have a draw chair, have your patient sit with their back straight, extend their arm so that there is a dip in the crook of their elbow, and place their forearm against the arm of the chair.

Position your body on the right side of the arm that you are drawing and face your patient. There will be a slight bend in your back depending on the height of the draw chair and the stature of your patient. If you are drawing your patient and they need to lie down, have them lay their arm flat on the bed or draw table about 45 degrees away from their side. Their hand should be about 1-2 feet away from their body, depending on the draw table size of the bed. Next, position your body facing the patient so that your left hip is closest to their hand. This will allow you a full range of motion to pull back with your left hand and stick the patient with your right hand.

Regarding plasma donation, your patient will have their body on a draw bed with an armrest for their draw arm. You will be able to move this armrest up and down and side to side to best fit your patient's body type and vein appearance. During plasma donation, the needle remains in the patient's arm, rather than just a plastic catheter, like with an IV. Due to this, the patient's arm needs to stay immobilized throughout the entire procedure. Failure to keep the arm in the same position can lead to infiltration and hematomas. This means that it is super important that your patient, otherwise known as a donor during plasma collection, is completely comfortable in the position they choose to be in.

Tip #3: Tying a Tourniquet

- Step 1- Hold the tourniquet perpendicular to the arm.
- Step 2- Place the tourniquet 3-6 inches above the intended place of draw underneath the patient's arm.
- Step 3- Pull the tourniquet toward you until both sides are taut against the back of the arm and either hand is at the same height.
- Step 4- Take your right hand and grab the tourniquet from the left hand, still holding the right side of the tourniquet secure.
- Step 5- With your left hand, take the right side of the tourniquet and cross it over top of the left side of the tourniquet. The tourniquet should now look like an x and still be taut.
- Step 6- Place your left thumb and index finger on the x of the tourniquet and let go with your right hand.
- Step 7- If your tourniquet is not making the skin pucker (scrunch together), use your right hand to pull the bottom side of the tourniquet away from the x until it is tight enough.
- Step 8- Take your index finger and push the excess length of the tourniquet through the opening between the x of the tourniquet and the patient's arm.
- Step 9- Let the x go against the skin and hold the excess material in place.
- Step 10- Grab the small tab at the top of the tie and pull it straight out; this will pop the tourniquet off.

Tip #4: Finding the Right Gloves for you

There are a lot of different gloves on the market, and each one will affect the way that you stick differently. At hospitals and certain clinics, you do not have a choice about what gloves you wear since they are uniform throughout the building. Typically, these gloves are smooth powder-free nitrile and are thin. Gloves need to be thin and smooth so we can feel the veins well enough to do an educated stick. Gloves are meant to be flush against the skin, not having any ripple in the top or fingers of the glove, but it is okay if they fit looser around the wrist as long as they stay on. A glove is too tight when it causes indentations on the wrist or restricts the range of motion in the fingers. Gloves come in sizes XS, S, M, L, and XL, and there are usually guides on the side of the box to recommend your size; however, the best way to tell is to try them on.

In outpatient laboratories, the types of gloves vary a lot. There are certain gloves that have ridges on them and are thicker, which makes it harder to find veins; gloves that aren't as thin and aren't true to size, causing them to be tighter and more restrictive; and also, many different colors of gloves. You will get a feel for your favorite type and size and eventually feel weird NOT wearing gloves. Gloves are your number one barrier between you and your patient and must always be worn when drawing a patient. When entering a room or before drawing a patient, utilize hand sanitizer, and if necessary, palpate your patient's arm before putting on gloves. If the patient has fluid present on the arm, open wounds, or a contagious virus, you need to have gloves on before you palpate.

Your number one job is to protect yourself so that you can continue to care for your patients. If a glove rips or tears, you must replace your gloves as soon as it is safe to. If you get a needle poke through a glove, thoroughly wash your hands, and use hand sanitizer before examining your hand to see if the needle stuck your skin. If your gloves become soiled before a stick, you must change them. This could be you touching your hair accidentally, fixing your mask, dropping your tube on the ground and picking it up, or touching your label printer. Your gloves must be clean before opening the skin of a patient to prevent the spread of diseases and infections. Gloves must also be worn when you are handing samples with blood, urine, stool, or other fluids on them.

After you use gloves, they must be thrown away in a biohazard bin because they have touched a patient and have been in contact with blood or fluids. In a hospital, all trash is handled as a potential biohazard, so the gloves can go right in the trash can. However, gloves, tourniquets, and all equipment that you take into psychiatric patients' rooms must be removed with you. You cannot leave anything in the room you go into other than the Band-Aid on the patient.

Be extremely vigilant when it comes to gloves because it seems so easy to remember, but it is the most significant part of patient safety and biohazard protocols. To safely remove soiled gloves, grab the glove of your opposite hand and pull it over your hand in one movement. Then take your bare hand and do the same thing on the other glove to avoid touching the soiled gloves, and both gloves are inside out by the time you are finished.

Tip #5: Learn Your Needle Types and Gauges

Vacutainers come in two gauges, 21 and 22. My favorite is the 21G, and if I see a vein that can't handle a 21G, then I usually just go for a 23G butterfly needle. The gauge is one of the factors that will determine how fast the blood is going to flow into the tube. It is not recommended to use a smaller gauge unless you really need to. 25G butterflies should be reserved for infants and small children or when you are attempting to stick a surface vein. These run extremely slowly and require precision to stay off of the sides of the vein that you are sticking. Once you get your flash using a butterfly, you need to keep the needle and your pull back hand extremely still so as not to jostle the vein. In a NICU setting, nurses will attach a 3mL syringe to a 25G needle and have one nurse hold the baby's arm, one nurse stick the baby and keep the needle still, and yet another nurse to slowly draw back on the syringe plunger. This is to minimize the possibility of error or vein damage. Consequentially, this is rarely possible for normal phlebotomists because there is an abundance of patients. Each phlebotomist draws patients alone and only returns to the lab with their coworkers when there are no draws at that time.

Lancets are much different than the venous draw needles because lancets eject a needle out from the top to pierce the skin and immediately sheath themselves. An adult lancet has a small needle and is used on fingertips only. Pediatric lancets are a square shape and eject a small blade that slices the heel to allow for a higher rate of flow to prevent clotting. Capillary draws also clot and stop bleeding extremely fast.

Tip #6: Eclipse Needles and How They Work

Eclipse needles come in 21G and 22G and are the most common needles used in phlebotomy. The 21G needle comes with a green lid that covers the needle end and a white cap that covers the rubber end that gets screwed into the hub base. A pink needle shield facing the green cap gets pushed over the needle at the end of the draw to protect the patient and the phlebotomist from getting stuck again. Under no circumstances should you ever use two hands to close a needle shield. However, since your thumb is already on the top of the hub when you are drawing your patient, you can push the needle shield on right as you pull the needle out of your patient.

The only difference between the 21G and 22G is the circumference of the needle, and instead of a green cap, the 22G has a black cap over the needle.

Tip #7: Order of Draw

The order of draw is important to remember so that the additives in each tube do not cross into ones that they are not supposed to. Every phlebotomist eventually gets the order down like the back of their hand. Below is a comprehensive list of the order to draw:

- Blood Cultures (Sterile Technique)
- Royal Blue SST and Royal Blue K2EDTA tubes for trace element testing
- Sodium Citrate tubes

- Red Top tubes
- SST tubes
- Lithium Heparin tubes and Sodium Heparin tubes
- K2EDTA and EDTA tubes
- Fluoride/Oxalate tubes
- TB Gold testing

Tip #8: What is in a Phlebotomists Draw Kit?

In a hospital, the phlebotomists are not drawing down in the lab in the draw chairs; therefore, they must take all their supplies with them. Some trays can either be carried or put on carts with wheels. Inside these trays is everything you would find in a regular draw room. This includes but is not limited to:

- **Heel Warmers**- Heel warmers are placed on the heels of infants before we poke them with a lancet to perform the newborn screen or collect a capillary sample from the heel. Looking much like hand warmers, these instantly heat when they are squeezed. These can also be used on extremely cold patients; therefore, the veins do not appear.
- **Capillary Tubes**- Capillary tubes are tubes used to collect the blood drops produced by a capillary stick. These tubes are either 700 microliters or 600 microliters big, depending on what sample needs to be taken. The only capillary tubes are SST tubes, PST tubes, K2EDTA tubes, and Red Top tubes.
- **Capillary Tube Extenders**- These are pieces of plastic that fit onto the end of capillary tubes to elongate them so that a sample label can be placed on when the labels are too large to fit solely on the capillary tube as is.
- **Common Draw Tubes**- These tubes are the ones typically ordered; we do not usually take rare tubes up since they take up our very limited space. If we do need rare tubes, we call the lab, and they send them up the tube system to the hospital area we are in. The common tubes that we carry are

the Lithium Heparin tubes, Red Top tubes, SST tubes, PST tubes, EDTA tubes, Blood Bank or K2EDTA tubes, and Sodium Citrate tubes.

- **Blood Culture Kits**- Adult blood culture kits are prepared in a biohazard bag. They contain two anaerobic bottles, two aerobic bottles, two iodine pads, two chloraprep pads, two 21G butterfly needles, two transfer devices, and two 20mL syringes.
- **Area Preparation Tools**- include alcohol wipes, iodine pads, chloraprep pads, and tourniquets.
- **5mL, 10mL, and 20mL syringes**- We keep all of these on hand in case we are called down to pull a trauma where you draw almost 60mL of blood. We also keep these on hand in the case of a difficult stick when you need to control the amount of pressure you exert against a particular vein so as not to blow it.
- **Gloves**- Some rooms only have medium and large gloves in the glove holders, so many phlebotomists will bring a handful of gloves with them in the pocket of their lab coat so they don't get stuck trying to find a pair when they are in a rush.
- **Biohazard Bags**- We carry around a stack of biohazard bags because all specimens need to be put in a biohazard bag (we call it a bios bag) before they are sent down to the lab.
- **Closures**- We keep paper tape, bandages, pediatric bandages, gauze, and Coban on us at all times. Paper tape is a roll of medical tape that is fast and easy but can easily tear delicate skin, so it has to be used with care. The bandages and pediatric bandages are used most of the time and placed over a folded gauze. Coban is the most hair and skin-friendly because it sticks to itself but leaves the skin that it is on relatively unharmed and maintains pressure to keep the vein closed.
- **Needles**- We keep mostly 21G vacutainer needles and hubs in our tray because it is what we use the most. We also make sure to keep some 21G, and 23G butterflies with us in case we need to use a syringe to draw or a vein is acting difficult

and is sideways. We don't use the 22G vacutainers at the hospital, but we do a lot at the clinic.

Tip #9: Labeling Specimens

As I explained earlier, there need to be two patient identifiers on each patient sample. This is the patient's date of birth in (mm/dd/yyyy) format and the patient's first and last names. The procedure is different for blood cultures. When labeling blood cultures, you need to know specific times. After you draw the first set (1 anaerobic and 1 aerobic bottle), you need to label them with the time drawn, date drawn, two patient identifiers, your initials, where you have drawn it from, and the amount of blood you put into the bottle. For example:

> MB   01/20/2021 1635
> Doe, John
> 10/16/1974
> Left AC   10 mL

This is necessary, so the doctor knows that if one set comes back normal and one set grows bacteria, it was something on the skin area where you drew, rather than being an infection or bacteria in the blood itself. So routine blood draws will be labeled simply:

> MB   01/20/2021 1635
> Doe, John
> 10/16/1974

The lab will discard the specimen if you do not have two patient identifiers or if your patient identifiers are illegible. It is for the patient's safety that a sample is not confused with another patient.

Types of Blood

Tip #10: What is a Vein? Venous Blood.

When performing typical blood draws, we opt for venous blood. If you look at your order—what tests the doctor wants to be performed on the blood—it will specify if the draw can be capillary or if it needs to be venous. This is extremely important in young children, whom we prefer to perform capillary draws on. Venous sticks are much more stressful on young children and tend to hurt slightly more. Veins are the transport system that brings deoxygenated blood back to the heart. Venous blood, being deoxygenated, is the typical dark red that we see on television. You can tell when you are palpating a vein when there is a bounce, and you can roll your fingertip side to side and feel both edges of the vein. If we imagine a vein like a straw, we want to stick the needle with the bevel up into the end of the straw, not through the side. We only want to stick the needle in until we get a flash. A flash occurs when the vacuum seal of a butterfly needle pulls blood from a vein into a narrow opening in the needle but doesn't continue to come out. Once we get a flash, we stop moving the needle and attach the tube to the vacutainer, which allows the tube to slowly fill with blood. If using a vacutainer, you determine whether or not you are in a vein by inserting a tube into the hub. If blood does not begin to flow into the tube, pull back the needle slowly and attempt to adjust your stick.

Tip #11: What is an Artery? Arterial Blood.

A typical phlebotomist will never stick an artery unless there is a dire necessity. At the hospital where I worked, arterial draws were done by the respiratory therapists (RTs). RTs would draw arterial blood gases, which provide the level of O_2 and CO_2 present in a patient's blood, to determine if they are oxygenating well enough as well as various other levels. This procedure is pretty painful, as a long needle is inserted in either a small artery in the wrist or a deep artery in the crook of the elbow. You can tell an artery from a vein by holding your finger on it lightly; if it is an artery, you will feel it pulsating. This is because arteries carry oxygenated blood from the heart to the tissue. If you are attempting to stick a vein and accidentally stick an artery, you will know by the color of the blood. Arterial blood being oxygenated creates a bright red color instead of the typical dark red color of venous blood. If this occurs, finish your collection if lab work does not specify between arterial and venous samples. After your collection, hold pressure on the puncture site for 5 minutes and then wrap in Coban. The Coban should be tight enough to maintain pressure but not too tight that it cuts off blood flow. Notify the nurse that you poked an artery instead of a vein by mistake and ask them to check the site for residual bleeding in an hour. It is significantly more problematic and potentially deadly for a nurse to place an IV in an artery.

Story Time:

While working in a hospital, I had to draw a patient in the surgery preparation area of PRE-OP. This patient was an older female who had very difficult veins. After checking both of her arms, I had stuck her twice with no luck. She had very fragile varicose veins that blew when I stuck them. Typically, people have their biggest vein be their antecubital vein (AC), which is in the middle of the crook of their elbow. She had what looked like a great vein there, but upon further inspection, I determined that it was her artery that was brought closer to the surface due to her low BMI (Body Mass Index).

After two unsuccessful attempts, I asked the nurse if I could wait and get my blood off of her IV start. An IV start is when a nurse starts an IV and pulls back blood before flushing it with saline to prepare it for medication. The nurse said, of course, and began to prepare what I had deemed to be an artery. I was very alarmed and notified the nurse that that was an artery, not a vein. She argued that she was more experienced than I was and proceeded to place an IV in it anyway, despite the patient being worried that I was correct. When placing an IV, there is a thin plastic tube called a catheter on the outside of the needle. Once there is a flash or a small amount of blood in the tubing, the nurse will advance the catheter by pushing it completely into the vein. Once the catheter is in place, the nurse will snap the needle out by pushing the safety button on the end of the needle. When the IV is in a vein, nothing will come out of the end of the catheter until either a syringe is placed on the end of the catheter to draw blood or the saline is attached to flush the vein. In this case, the IV was placed in an artery, and once the needle was pulled out of the catheter, blood immediately gushed out of the end and pooled onto the floor.

The nurses were quick to apply gauze to the IV stick and pulled the catheter out. At this point, I had to excuse myself from the room, and the patient had to be evaluated for how much blood was lost. This is one of the reasons why teamwork in this profession is of the utmost importance. Just because you believe something to be true does not mean that it is. Take all advice seriously before you potentially endanger your patient. For example, if the nurse were to have administered a saline flush through the artery, there would be a large potential for a pseudoaneurysm or hematoma, and it would cause immense pain to your patient. Certain medications can also cause blockages or necrosis in the tissues of the body if they are administered into an artery.

Tip #12: What are Capillaries? Capillary Blood.

Capillary blood is also deoxygenated and will look very similar to venous blood, which is that dark red color. Since capillary blood collection is much slower than venous blood collection, we must make sure to do it correctly to prevent it from clotting. This process will be explained later on. Capillary blood is what we see when we get a paper cut or scrape our knee, it is that first layer under our skin. You can tell a lot by looking at a person's capillaries. For example, nurses and paramedics will check your capillary refill when they are treating you. A capillary refill check is when you pinch someone's fingertip, release it, and count to see how long until the blood flows back to the phalange. This will indicate if you are having trouble circulating or perfusing your blood; both can be symptoms of major problems. Capillary draws are either done on a fingertip or on the heels of infants who do not yet walk. The puncture site clots over very fast, so typically, you should only be extracting the blood for 1-3 minutes to get a good sample.

Types of Veins

Tip #13: Rolling Veins

When attempting to find a good vein in a patient's arm, it is all about the bounce. This is how we differentiate between muscle, tendon, bone, vein, and artery. Rolling veins occur when a nurse or a phlebotomist attempts to stick a needle into a vein, and the vein moves from its original position. To prevent this, phlebotomists will use the thumb on their opposite hand and pull it back on the skin to secure the vein in place. In very rare circumstances, the vein rolls despite being pulled back. We know if a vein rolls away because there will not be a flash, and the tubes will not fill with blood. If a vein rolls away from the needle, the phlebotomist will palpate above the needle to locate the vein again. Once they find the vein again, they will secure it in place again by pulling back with their thumb, they will then slowly turn the needle and advance it forward until the blood starts to fill the tube or they get a flash. We typically only "dig around" for up to 20 seconds as long as the patient is still comfortable and not in much pain. If the patient exhibits pain right away, we will ask if they would like us to move the needle or take it out and stick a different vein or arm. Moving the needle around needs to be done very carefully to prevent infiltration and discomfort to the patient.

Tip #14: Hand Veins

Hand veins are more painful for blood draws and IVs than arm veins by far. This is because there are significantly more nerves on the top of your hand than in the crook of your elbow. There is also less fatty tissue and a greater likelihood that the needle can strike bone. They tend to be more likely to roll and disappear than antecubital veins are, but they can be a great option, especially for patients with IVs present in their antecubital veins. Additionally, patients going through vaginal labor and delivery cannot have IVs in their antecubital veins because of the bending of their arms. Since the catheters that IVs have are flexible plastic tubing, they are able to be bent and moved around and still be viable. However, if they are bent too much or for too long, the medicine is not able to get through and into the vein. Once the IV pump detects that there is a blockage or a kink in the catheter or the rest of the tubing, it will stop pushing medication and alarm that it is occluded.

Hand veins in elderly patients also tend to be more prominent and visible than their antecubital veins. Skin tears more easily in people who are elderly, and their veins heal a lot slower, so it is imperative to stick them carefully. Bruises are much more common in this population as well. It is never ideal for sticking a bruised vein because it has already been damaged and needs to heal. They will also be more painful to the patient and take longer to draw because blood will run more slowly. An intriguing thing about blowing hand veins is that you can watch it happen more clearly. You can also see antecubital veins blow in young children, very skinny patients, and elderly patients with translucent-like skin. If I advance the needle in and blow the vein, I can see the blood seep out of the vein and into the surrounding areas, which creates a nasty-looking bruise.

Tip #15: *Most Common Arm Veins*

Most phlebotomists won't know exactly what vein they are sticking, other than the median antecubital vein. The most common spot to draw blood from is the median antecubital vein because it is in the middle of the crook of the elbow and is usually the largest. However, the basilic vein is sometimes more prominent and feels stronger than the median antecubital. The basilic vein is located on the side of the antecubital vein in the crook of the elbow. The cephalic vein is on the opposite side of the median antecubital vein than the basilic vein is and is typically very angled and hard to reach with any needle other than a 23G butterfly needle. Higher up in the arm are brachial veins, but like hand veins, those are only reserved for when there is no luck in drawing blood from the most common veins. Additionally, if there is no luck in drawing blood from a critically ill patient for a long time, the doctor will sign off on having the phlebotomist draw blood from the top of the foot.

Tip #16: Surface Veins

A surface vein is a vein that is visible without a tourniquet and is extremely small. These veins are not suitable for blood collection on a large scale but can be attempted if there are no other viable veins. Surface veins are too small for IVs to be placed and most times will blow even with a standard 23G butterfly needle. For veins to be viable for blood collection, they need to be able to handle the pressure that a needle will put on the vein and the size of the needle itself. Even with the smallest needle, there is still the likelihood that all attempts to stick a surface vein will just blow and cause a bruise.

There are devices used that radiate red light or ultrasound that allow us to see the inside of a patient's arms when we cannot feel any veins. This typically is found in heavier patients when their veins are hidden under thick layers of fatty tissue. Surface veins appear all over when you use these devices, and they enable you to choose the largest surface vein to attempt to draw.

Chapter Review

- Following the correct safety techniques in phlebotomy is the essence of this profession. We want all of our patients to feel safe and comfortable and go through as little pain as possible to get their blood drawn. Therefore, the tourniquet techniques should be followed to prevent markings on the patient's arms, to prevent veins from being damaged, and skin blistering. In addition, glove protocols should be followed to avoid cross-contamination and the spread of diseases.

- The correct needles should be used to draw blood from veins to prevent damage to veins. Butterfly needles need to be used with delicate and small veins, and the correct techniques should be used to preserve vein function throughout the draw. While making the right needle choice, the correct veins should also be chosen to prevent excessive blood loss and poking of the patient.
- Patient labeling and identifiers are extremely fundamental as they are used to prevent patient mix-ups and sample mix-ups. For example, if we have a patient who has trouble with clotting and we mix up their blood work and don't get them their heparin, it could be potentially fatal. On the other side, giving a patient potassium when they don't need it can induce a heart attack in extreme cases. The list goes on and on. So always ensure you have the correct patient and that you are labeling clearly and accurately.
- Be sure to use patience and caution when sticking hand veins and rolling veins. It is extremely painful for the patient to have the needle moving around in their arm, especially in their hand. Adjusting the needle in a hand comes with such a high likelihood of damaging nerves, striking bone, and blowing veins. It should be done gingerly and should stop when the patient exhibits more than normal discomfort or if they ask you to stop.
- If you are drawing patients in a hospital, keep more than the necessary materials in your draw kit. There are going to be times when you may have to call down to the lab for foil on a light-sensitive sample, but you don't want to be waiting for 10 minutes for a 20mL syringe during a sepsis alert. Many phlebotomists prefer to use carts since you can attach extra bins to the neck and store extra supplies. Be sure to stock additionals of the needles you are most comfortable using; otherwise, you'll run out and be stuck using the needles you took just to be safe.

Chapter 2: Sample Collection and Processing

Key terms in this chapter: Chemistry, Microbiology, Hematology, Cytology, Clotting, Specimens, and Minimums.

Chemistry Lab Work

Tip #17: Serum Separator Tubes (Tiger Top versus Gold Top) (SST)

Serum separator tubes have a layer of clot activator and serum separator gel. The tests that are run off of SST tubes are not blood tests but rather serum tests. This means that before we can run these tests on the samples, the serum must be separated from the red blood cells. The clot activator makes the whole sample become one thick clot in the tube, and when it starts to visibly separate, it is ready for the centrifuge. It takes 15-25 minutes for the serum separator to work, so it must sit until a small amount of liquid seeps out from the clot in the tube that is a light red tint. At this point, we can put the tube in the centrifuge across from a vial of water that is the same weight relatively as the blood sample. This is to keep the centrifuge balanced and spin the way we want it to. We will centrifuge it for 10 minutes, regardless of how many samples we put in.

My centrifuge is small and can hold six tubes at a time. Once it is done spinning, there should be a light yellowish-brown serum floating on the top and a clot of red blood cells down at the bottom. Blood serum is derived from this process and is distinctly different than plasma since the blood clotted first and was separated by centrifuging. Red and black top tiger tubes are 10ml large and exert harsher pressure on the vein when drawing; a gold top is 6ml and exerts less pressure on veins. Both are used in our clinic setting, but only gold tops are used at our hospital.

The most common tests that I see drawn with these tubes are:

- Cortisol (can be drawn normally or ordered within 30 minutes of 0800)
- hCG (Human chorionic gonadotropin) (drawn during a pregnancy confirmation protocol)
- FSH(Follicle Stimulating Hormone)/LH (Luteinizing Hormone)
- Glucose Tolerance (should be drawn on a patient fasting for at least 8 hours)
- CMP (Comprehensive Metabolic Panel)/BMP (Basic Metabolic Panel)
- Lipid Panel (should be drawn on a patient fasting for at least 8 hours)

Tip #18: *Plasma Separator Tubes (PST)*

Plasma separator tubes are relatively similar to serum separator tubes but differ in size, color, and product. PST tubes draw the plasma out of blood while it is not clotted. There is a coagulant and a plasma separator gel at the bottom of the 3.5mL tube. While the majority of the tubes I use at the clinic are SSTs, hospitals prefer the PST instead. These tubes are much thinner with a plastic top instead of a rubber top like the tiger top. There will be a lot number and an expiration number as always. If your clinic does not use them often, you must always check the expiration date. It will also have the reference number, manufacturer's name, amount of chemicals that are present in the tube, and what chemicals are inside the tube. The amount of chemicals in the tube is measured as a USP unit. The units are mass-based on the expected effects they will have on the blood biologically.

The most common tests that I see drawn with these tubes are:

- CMP (Comprehensive Metabolic Panel)/BMP (Basic Metabolic Panel)

- Hepatic Function Panel
- Ammonia (Must be put on ice immediately and transferred to the lab)
- Ionized Calcium

Tip #19: Clot Activator Tubes (Red Top tubes)

Clot activator tubes (or red tops) are not commonly used. These tubes are 10mL and look exactly like a tiger top tube, except for the black on the stopper and there not being any gel in the bottom of the tube. There is no USP listed on the tube since there is no additive in the tube. It is not necessary to invert it since it is meant to clot, and there are no additives.

The most common tests that I see drawn with these tubes are:

- Rheumatoid Factor (Can also be drawn in an SST, PST, or EDTA)
- RPR (Can also be drawn in an SST, PST, or EDTA)
- Uric Acid (Can also be drawn in an SST or a PST)
- Amylase (Can also be drawn in an SST or a PST)
- Prealbumin (Can also be drawn in an SST)
- Magnesium (Can also be drawn in a Navy Blue EDTA or SST)
- Cortisol (Can also be drawn in an SST)
- Lipase (Can also be drawn in an SST or a Lithium Heparin)

Tip #20: Lithium Heparin/Sodium Heparin Tubes

Lithium heparin tubes have a dark green top and come in sizes of 3.5ml, 6ml, and 9ml. They are each coated with lithium heparin on the inside; each has a different USP as they all allow for different volumes of blood to be drawn. For example, the 3.5ml has a USP of 75, the 6ml has a USP of 95, and the 9ml has an unlisted USP. The 9ml lithium heparin tubes are used mainly for a TSPOT test, otherwise known as a tuberculosis test. Lithium is a chemical element that is an alkali metal and is mainly used as psychiatric treatment medication in an array of lithium compounds called lithium salts. Sodium is another element, as well as an alkali metal, which is also a salt. Heparin comes in the form of either sodium heparin or lithium heparin. Heparin is an anticoagulant and is used in the treatment of blood clots and certain blood disorders. Lithium heparin tubes can give false high results in lithium testing used to diagnose bipolar disorder, whereas sodium heparin tubes can give false high results in sodium level testing. However, it is generally more common to use lithium heparin tubes to test electrolytes, most notably lactate. Lithium heparin tubes are also the best for electrolyte testing because of their low cation concentration and ability to not interfere with water solubility. Since the biological agent is sprayed onto the sides of the tube in manufacturing, it is necessary to invert the tube multiple times to get the agent to mix with the blood sample. Inverting is simply tilting the tube up and down at a moderate speed. Shaking a sample is never good or okay; this will cause hemolysis, and your sample will be marked as insufficient in the lab and need to be redrawn. Sodium heparin tubes are used to prepare heparinized plasma and whole blood for a variety of laboratory testing.

The most common tests that I see drawn with these tubes are:

- Lactic Acid- Whole Blood (do not put on ice) (3.5ml tube)
- Lactic Acid (must be put on ice after being drawn) (3.5ml tube)
- Lactate (must be put on ice after being drawn) (3.5ml tube)
- Whole Blood Calcium (3.5ml tube) (must be put on ice immediately)
- Vitamin B12 (must be wrapped in foil to prevent light exposure to sample) (some laboratories prefer using an SST to test Vitamin B12)
- TSPOT (this is a one-time blood test used to test tuberculosis)

Tip #21: Trace Element Serum Tubes

We very rarely see these tubes drawn, but they are used when there is suspected exposure to a toxic material such as lead, copper, arsenic, and mercury. This is most commonly drawn on babies and toddlers at their 1-year and 2-year checkups if there are unusual findings. Most times, on kids this young, we can draw a capillary sample using a K2EDTA tube. When we do have to draw a venous lead, there are two options: a NavyBlue K2EDTA tube with 10.8mg being 6ml or a NavyBlue serum without a given USP.

You must submit the patient demographics form for public health reporting with these tubes. This is in case their blood is positive for a contaminant so that the exposure can be dealt with through the proper channels. For example, lead used to be commonly used in paint until they found out it was toxic and banned it, but there are still many houses where lead paint has been forgotten about. Also, countries outside the US have different protocols about contaminants, and merchandise coming from overseas can yield harmful ingredients or parts.

The most common tests that I see drawn with these tubes are:

- Lead (Venous)
- Copper, Serum or Plasma (If the patient is taking nutritional supplements, they should discontinue use before testing to minimize confounding variables)
- Mercury (Whole Blood) (If the patient is taking nutritional supplements, they should discontinue use prior to testing to minimize confounding variables. Testing should occur immediately as mercury is a volatile element and the concentration initially present in the blood may decrease over time.)

Hematology Lab Work

Tip #22: K2 EDTA Tubes

K2EDTA tubes or 'blood bank tubes' are used mainly for blood-related tests such as typing and transfusion medicine. K2 is a variety of EDTA tubes known as dipotassium EDTA. EDTA stands for ethylenediaminetetraacetic acid, which almost no phlebotomists know how to say or spell. It is a type of strong anticoagulant that keeps the red blood cells from clotting so that testing can be performed on them. EDTA itself is insoluble in water and works by binding to the calcium present in the blood to prevent it from clotting. The USP in a K2 EDTA tube is 10.8mg or 1.8mg of EDTA per 1 milliliter of whole blood.

The most common tests that I see drawn with these tubes:

- ABO and RH Type (used during new OB workups to determine if the mother needs the Rhogam shot)
- Antibody Screen (RBC Antibody screen is drawn immediately before getting the Rhogam shot)
- Type and Screen (Drawn when a patient requires blood in a hospital and before a patient delivers a baby in case blood is required)
- Crossmatch

Tip #23: EDTA Whole Blood Tubes

EDTA tubes simply have the ethylenediaminetetraacetic acid instead of having the dipotassium in it as well. This acid is a strong anticoagulant. Most tests that are performed in a K2EDTA can be performed in an EDTA, but a K2EDTA is still preferred. The reason that a K2EDTA is preferred is due to the anticoagulant properties being stronger, preventing clotting. This is why we only use K2EDTA tubes when drawing capillary labs that are typically done in a regular EDTA. However, if a patient's venous sample continues to clot in an EDTA, we may attempt to run the test in a K2EDTA.

Furthermore, if a test meant for a K2EDTA ends up being run in an EDTA, there is not much of a difference as long as the sample does not clot. There are 10mL EDTA tubes, but the majority are only 4mL. The K2EDTA tubes, however, are 6mL.

The most common tests that I see drawn with these tubes:

Complete Blood Count (Only needs 400 micrograms to run)

Hemoglobin (This is super important since hemoglobin under 6 requires a blood transfusion)

Hemoglobin A1C +est (with estimated) Glucose (Insurance doesn't typically cover this test more than once every 90 days, so a patient needs to sign an ABN)

Sedimentation Rate (Requires a minimum of 1.0 mL of blood)

Tip #24: Sodium Fluoride/Sodium Oxalate Tubes

NaF (Sodium Fluoride) or $Na_2C_2O_4$ (Sodium Oxalate) tubes are used for their antiglycolytic properties. This property inhibits glycolysis, which is the process of the body breaking down glucose in the bloodstream. Therefore, the glucose is the most accurate and present in the blood by stopping the blood from continuing to process the glucose. Similarly, police use sodium fluoride tubes to perform blood alcohol content testing since they have to take the blood with them and log it into evidence. The additive in this tube prevents the blood from breaking down the alcohol and reducing the blood alcohol content that eventually is found in the blood. Unfortunately, we do not do blood alcohol testing at the hospital, which may take multiple hours to perform. You must also invert the tube at least eight times to ensure that the additive mixes with the blood and does what it is meant to do.

The most common tests that I see with these tubes:

- Glucose
- Blood Alcohol Content (follow police procedures strictly)
- Lactic Acid (must be on ice)

Tip #25: *Sodium Citrate Tubes*

$Na_3C_6H_5O_7$ (Sodium Citrate) tubes are used for coagulation testing. The blood to the additive ratio for these tubes is nine parts blood to 1 part sodium citrate, with the tube containing 0.109 M, 3.2% sodium citrate. M is a symbol in chemistry that stands for molarity. Molarity is the concentration of a chemical, which makes sense when the tubes have a 9:1 blood to additive ratio. All sodium citrate tubes have two protruding lines near the top of the tube. These lines signify the amount of blood that is required. If a sample is collected and the blood is below the bottom line, the lab will reject the sample and order a redraw. The lines are at 70% of the volume of the tube, which is 2.7mL large, and the sample must be within +/- 10% of the minimum sample required. The difficulty with sodium citrate tubes is that the vacuum exhausts before the minimum blood required is fulfilled within the tube, causing another tube to be drawn. This is why I prefer to draw using a syringe and a butterfly and transfer the blood into the tube with a transfer device, so I can advance more blood into the tube when the vacuum ceases to pull blood in naturally. Otherwise, you need to use a waste tube, which can only be a red top or a red and white waste tube. Sodium citrate tubes cannot have any other tubes drawn before them other than the red top tubes since those do not have additives. Since a sodium citrate tube measures the coagulation properties of a patient's blood, it would be detrimental to draw an EDTA tube before the sodium citrate. This is due to the anticoagulant present in the EDTA tube presenting a potential contamination risk to my sodium citrate blood sample and making it invalid.

The most common tests that I see with these tubes:

- aPTT (activated partial thromboplastin time)
- PTT (partial thromboplastin time)

Tip #26: Trace Element K2EDTA

While I touched on trace element tubes in the prior section regarding trace element tubes, there are a few differences between the serum trace element tubes and the K2EDTA trace element tubes. Much like the regular K2EDTA tubes, the additive is the dipotassium ethylenediaminetetraacetic acid, and the serum tube does not contain anything and is just the clot activator tube. The K2EDTA metal transport tubes are specifically meant for the trace element tubes that must be tested on whole blood. The serum metal transport tubes are specifically meant for trace element tubes that must be tested on serum. It is very important to look at the label on the NavyBlue tubes since that is the only way to tell which type of tube it is.

The most common tests that I see with these tubes:

- Aluminum
- Zinc

Cytology Lab Work

Tip #27: Urine Samples

There are a lot of different ways that we collect standard urine samples. For example, there is routine void (dirty catch), catheterized urine collection, midstream clean catch, and infant and pediatric collections.

A routine void is when a doctor orders a urine sample to be collected into a urine cup and does not specify that the patient must first clean themselves before voiding. This may be ordered with a comment stating the sample must be taken 2 hours after voiding to ensure a dirty sample. This ensures that the specimen contains the surface bacteria of the penis or vagina that may not occur within the urine itself but on the genitalia. For a urine culture, minute samples are acceptable down to just a few drops. For a urinalysis, more urine is required for the testing.

A catheterized urine collection is when a patient has a tube inserted into their urethra that drains their urine directly from their bladder to the bag, most commonly called a foley catheter. Now, suppose a patient has an epidural during labor and does not have a foley catheter. In that case, the nurses may opt to use straight catheterizing techniques, which drain the bladder immediately, and then the tube is removed. In a hospital, the nurse will perform the urine collection and send it down to the lab. However, if a patient comes down to the outpatient lab and they are unable to retrieve a sample from their bag, we must assist them in draining it into a cup. Only perform this task if you are aware of how to do it and if you maintain sanitary conditions. If you are unsure what to do, call a nurse or a coworker for help.

A midstream clean catch is the most common type of urine collection. It calls for a patient to use a Castille Soap Towelette to wipe their genitalia thoroughly before voiding into the cup. This is to ensure that no surface bacteria get into the sample and gives incorrect results.

For women:

- Wash your hands thoroughly
- Open the urine cup without touching the inside
- Spread labia apart and wipe from front to back with the Castille soap towelette. If there is still discharge or debris, wipe again with a new wipe.
- Begin to urinate into the toilet.
- Place the cup underneath the stream after voiding some urine.

- Collect as much urine as you can into the cup.
- Clean the cup off, wash your hands, and give your sample to the phlebotomist.

For men:

- Wash your hands thoroughly.
- Open the urine cup without touching the inside.
- Pull back your foreskin or any skin obstructing the urinary opening.
- Use the Castille wipe to clean the entire tip of your penis.
- Begin to urinate into the toilet.
- Place the cup into the stream after voiding some urine.
- Collect as much urine as you can into the cup.
- Clean the cup off, wash your hands, and give your sample to the phlebotomist.

If you get a sample into the cup, even if it is just a few drops, do not discard it! Chances are it is just enough for the laboratory testing; your phlebotomist will let you know.

Pediatric urine collections are somewhat difficult. We never want to have to put a catheter in them just to get a sample since there is a high risk of infection. Our first attempt is always securing a bag over their genitalia. The edges of the bag are attached around their genitalia with a hypoallergenic adhesive so that when they do void, it is collected in the bag and does not leak. The bag should be changed every 30 minutes or until the child voids. This technique is used for neonates to toddlers until they can sit on a toilet and void themselves with assistance from their parents. However, many times they attempt to pull these bags off, or there is an accidental leak that sets back the collection time.

Tip #28: Respiratory Samples

The most common respiratory sample is a respiratory swab. A respiratory swab is collected by inserting a Q-tip-like swab into either the back of a patient's nose or the back of a patient's throat. When inserted in the back of the nose, it is called a nasopharyngeal swab. If it is performed in the throat, it is simply a throat swab. Unfortunately, some unlucky patients get a dual nasopharyngeal/throat swab. Performing a complete respiratory panel on these swabs tests for the DNA or RNA of common bacteria or viruses that affect a patient's respiratory system. These viruses and bacteria are present in but not limited to COVID-19, Strep Throat, Flu, Rhinovirus, Human Metapneumovirus, or Bronchitis.

Other than swabs, a respiratory sample may be a sputum sample, nasal aspirates, nasal washes, bronchoalveolar lavage, bronchial wash, tracheal aspirate, and lung tissue. The most common are the sputum sample, nasal aspirate, and nasal wash.

- A sputum sample is a thick snot-like fluid that is found and made in the lungs. We take sputum samples to test if there is any fungus or bacteria present that is causing a patient's symptoms.
- A nasal aspirate is a catheter inserted into the naras while a nurse administers suction using a special trap apparatus. The trap will contain any secretions that are removed from the suction procedure to be sent to the lab for viral testing.
- A nasal wash is a procedure where a nurse administers a large amount of fluid into both nostrils with your head tilted back at 70 degrees. During this procedure, you close off your throat by flexing your tongue to the roof of your mouth. Once all of the fluid is in your nose, you will sit forward forcefully and blow all of the liquid into a petri dish for the laboratory.

Tip #29: Tuberculosis Testing

There are three ways to perform tuberculosis testing: TB Gold. TB Gold is a test that requires four tubes to contain 1 ml of blood each. The order is the grey top, green top, yellow top, and then the purple top. This tests for the antigens for TB1 and TB2. It is helpful when detecting mycobacterium tuberculosis.

- T Spot. The T spot test is a one-time blood draw of two large lithium heparin tubes to test for effector T cells that have been activated by mycobacterium tuberculosis.
- TB Skin test. This is a test that is performed by a nurse using an injection and observation method. For example, a nurse will inject a small amount of tuberculin under your skin in your forearm and instruct you to come back for your test to be read in 48 to 72 hours. These are not performed by phlebotomists.

Tuberculosis is an airborne contagious disease and must be handled with proper precautions. If a patient is suspected of TB, they must be in an isolated room that is vacuum controlled, and the phlebotomist must be wearing the proper PPE, including a PAPR, a gown, gloves, and shoe covers.

Tip #30: 24 Hour Urine Collections

A 24-hour urine is typically done in patients with abnormal laboratory tests or symptoms of kidney problems, such as urinalysis with the presence of protein or creatine in their urine. During a 24-hour urine, a patient will void their bladder when they want to begin and not collect that urine. You will mark the time you voided and then collect every urine into the jug until it has been 24 hours. For example, if I void my bladder into the toilet at 8:00 am, I will then collect my first urine in the jug the next time I use the bathroom at 11:00 am. After that, I will continue collecting my urine in the jug until 8:00 am the following day. Patients will receive a urine hat, a white plastic tool that they place under the seat of their toilet but out of the water and urinate into it. They will then take the urine in the hat and pour it into the jug. The jug must have the date and time started and ended, the patient's name, and the patient's birthday to be accepted.

Genetics

Tip #31: Genetic Testing Kits

There are many different genetics kits and commercial genetics companies. I will outline the three companies we work with the most at our laboratory.

- **Myriad Genetic Laboratories**: Myriad has a heredity cancer screening (called MyRisk) and prenatal screening (called Prequel). These are the two tests that we perform at the clinic. They are not performed at the hospital typically because they check for nonemergent chromosomal abnormalities. For the Prequel, these are abnormalities such as Trisomy 18 and 21 (down syndrome). In addition, emergent genetic testing, such as testing for alveolar capillary dysplasia, is not performed in these NIPS (noninvasive prenatal screening). It is classified as noninvasive in comparison to amniocentesis, which is invasive genetic testing that takes a sample of the amniotic fluid for further testing. The MyRisk screen will show if a patient has the ovarian or breast cancer genes, which does not mean they will get cancer, but just that it is a possibility.
- **Invitae Genetic Laboratories**: Invitae also has a NIPS test that is a little bit cheaper than some of the other options and still tests for the common chromosomal abnormalities and works as early as ten weeks. In addition, Invitae, like all of the other NIPS testing, allows you to find out the gender of your child with a 99% accuracy at ten weeks as well.
- **Natera Genetic Laboratories**: Natera has NIPT testing as well called Panorama. In addition, Natera has carrier screens to see if the mother is a carrier for diseases such as Tay Sachs and

Duchenne Muscular Dystrophy, called Horizon carrier screen. It also has additional panels that are ethnicity-specific such as Pan-ethnic Medium additional 13 genes available.

These tests are a big relief for parents who are nervous for their unborn children and for women with a history of genetic problems and cancers in their families. Unfortunately, a lot of the time, they can be extremely pricey, but insurance may cover it in some circumstances.

The common procedure for genetic lab work is the patient brings in a "kit," which is a box that includes instructions for the phlebotomist, a FedEx or shipping bag, a shipping label, a patient demographic form, an insurance card copy, the tubes needed, padding for the tubes, and interior packaging.

When I draw a Natera prequel, for example, there are two tubes inside a cloth sheath, which is inside a gel pack wrapped in a type of foil exterior. There is also a FedEx bag that says, "Exempt Human Specimen," and instructions for the collection. After I take the tubes out and fill them, I write my two patient identifiers and the date on the tube, put them back in the sheath, and place that in a biohazard bag with the patient demographics sheet and a copy of the insurance card. I then put the entire bag into the gel pack, pull off the paper strip, and secure both sides of the gel pack together. I then put the gel back inside the box it came in, put the box inside the FedEx bag, and fasten it shut. It is then picked up by our courier and sent to the company for processing.

Microbiology Lab Work

Tip #32: Stool Samples

Stool samples are collected in kits that include three tubes (an orange, a green, and a white one). These tubes each have different additives, just as blood tubes do. The white tube has no additives and is called the "clean" tube. It is used to test for C. difficle, white blood counts, red blood counts, O and P testing, Rotavirus, and Occult blood testing. The orange tube is called the "C &S" tube. It has a preservative additive and is used for stool cultures, Giardia/Cryptosporidium antigen testing, and E. Coli Shiga Toxin testing. The green tube is the "Ecofix" tube. It has a preservative additive and is used for O and P testing along with the white tube.

To collect stool samples, you must stool into a urine hat to make sure that it is a satisfactory sample. You will then use the built-in spoons on the caps of the tubes to scoop 2-3ml of stool into each tube. There are fill lines on each tube that you must use for reference to ensure that you have collected enough sample. If the specimen is liquid, fill the vials halfway. All vials must be filled within an hour of stooling into the urine hat and refrigerated immediately.

When submitting a stool sample, know that it is completely ordinary and routine for us and that nobody should be ashamed of it. This is a very important step in diagnosing GI (gastrointestinal) issues before a colonoscopy.

Tip #33: Blood Cultures

Blood cultures are very taxing for the patient but are extremely important for correctly diagnosing certain fungi and bacteria. To perform blood culture collections on adults, you will need:

- 2 chloraprep swabs
- 4 alcohol pads
- 2 anaerobic culture bottles
- 2 aerobic culture bottles
- 2 21 G butterfly needles
- 2 20mL syringes
- 2 iodine swabs OR 2 additional chloraprep swabs
- 1 tourniquet
- 2 gauze

- 2 transfer devices
- 1 roll of Coban
- 1 biohazard bag

To perform blood culture collections, follow the steps below:

- Inform the patient that to draw blood cultures, you will need to stick them twice and take a large quantity of blood (40 mL).
- Use your tourniquet to determine two viable veins for collection. These must be on different appendages if possible.
- Place all four bottles on the counter, one set will be one aerobic and one anaerobic bottle from one stick, and the other set will be from the other stick.
- You will either prep the bottles by popping the caps off and placing a drop of iodine over the top of the bottle and then placing an alcohol pad on top of them until the time of transfer. Or you will clean off the lids with a chloraprep swab and then place an alcohol pad on top of them until the time of transfer.
- You will use an alcohol wipe followed by a chloraprep pad to prepare the patient's vein. Repeat this step on the other venipuncture site as well after filling the first set of culture bottles and labeling them.
- Once you stick the patient, draw out 20 mL of blood into the syringe. Repeat this step on the other venipuncture site as well after filling the first set of culture bottles and labeling them.
- Once you wrap the patient's arm with Coban, use a transfer device to push 10mL of blood into each bottle in the first set (1 anaerobic and 1 aerobic).
- Label each bottle with which arm was used (left or right), where you stuck (AC, hand, wrist, etc.), how much you put in the bottle (10mL), the time you drew it (1405), the patients two identifiers (name and birthday), your initials, and the date. Repeat this step on the other venipuncture site after completion.

Chapter Review

- Blood is drawn into tubes with certain additives to aid in the testing that doctors require. These tubes are:
- SSTs (Serum Separator Tubes) (Tiger Top or Gold Top Tubes)
- PSTs (Plasma Separator Tubes) (Plasma Serum Separator Tubes)
- Clot Activators (Red Top Tubes)
- Lithium Heparin (Dark Green Tubes)
- EDTA (ethylenediaminetetraacetic acid) (Dark Purple Top Tubes)
- K2EDTA (dipotassium ethylenediaminetetraacetic acid) (Pink Top Tubes)
- Trace Element K2EDTA or Serum Tubes (Navy Blue Top Tubes)
- Sodium Fluoride or Sodium Oxalate Tubes (Grey Top Tubes)
- Sodium Citrate Tubes (Light Blue Top Tubes)
- TB Gold Tubes (Grey, Green, Yellow, Purple)
- Blood, urine, and stool samples must be collected in such a manner that does not contaminate the sample and obscure test results.
- Only medical professionals should perform advanced respiratory sample collections such as bronchial lavage, nasal wash, lung tissue biopsy, etc.
- Tuberculosis testing is necessary for immigrants attempting to gain citizenship in the country, employees entering a new job, and anyone suspected of having TB.
- Labs such as genetic testing and blood culture collections have a very specific process that needs to be followed; otherwise, the testing may not be accurate, or the lab will refuse the sample as they are incorrect.

Chapter 3: Staple Laboratory Tests and Panels

Key terms in this chapter: Fasting, Indicators, Glucola, and Hormones.

Routine Tests Performed During or Before Pregnancy

Tip #34: 1 Hour Glucose Testing

One-hour glucose tests are the mandatory testing performed on almost every pregnant woman between week 20 and week 28 of their pregnancy. Although, if patients are late to care, they could take their glucose test much later. If a patient has had gestational diabetes in previous pregnancies or has other risk factors, a doctor may order an additional one-hour test very early in the pregnancy. A one-hour glucose test involves a patient consuming a 50g glucola drink or an approved substitute in 5 minutes or less.

Most doctors recommend fasting for this test, as anything you consume will alter your results, especially sugar-heavy food or drink. The glucola we offer patients is 10 oz or 296mL and is fruit punch flavored. Some people object to drinking the red dye and opt to bring a substitute that has been approved by their doctor. In this case, patients still must finish the alternative drink in under 5 minutes. The purpose of having patients drink this in the allotted time is to improve the accuracy of the results. After 5 minutes, the patient's body starts to process the glucose where the time is not yet being recorded.

Once a patient finishes the drink, they wait an hour before getting drawn by the phlebotomist. I typically draw a one-hour glucose tolerance test with a hemoglobin or a CBC since the doctors want to check their hemoglobin. Some patients, especially those that are not used to sugary drinks, may get extremely nauseous and vomit. If a patient vomits or has to eat something to stave off nausea, the test has to be over, and they either have to repeat the test or submit to glucose testing until the end of their pregnancy.

Tip #35: 2 Hour Glucose Testing

Two-hour glucose tolerance testing is performed much less often than either the 1 hour or the 3-hour testing. It is performed on patients who exhibit abnormal symptoms or lab results postpartum. This testing ensures that a patient who developed gestational diabetes has not developed type 2 diabetes from pregnancy. For a 2-hour glucose tolerance test, a patient must be fasting for at least 8 hours when they arrive. This means not consuming anything other than plain water. Patients sometimes will confuse fasting with only drinking fluids, but you should not consume anything other than water for at least 8 hours and at most 16 hours before your test. When you get to the lab for your test, your blood will be drawn immediately and tested to see if your glucose is at an adequate level for testing (between 70 and 140 mg/dl). If you are fasting for longer, it may be lower, and if you have been fasting for a short period of time, it may be higher. Once your glucose level is confirmed, you are given a 75g glucola (also 296mL or 10oz), and ours tastes like orange soda. After finishing the drink, you will wait for two hours and then be drawn again. Every doctor has their own limit, but typically any glucose level over 140 is abnormal for a non-diabetic woman two hours after drinking the glucola.

There is also a 2-hour post-prandial glucose tolerance test. This test is just a one-time draw approximately two hours after eating a meal and then remaining stationary until after the blood draw is performed. The meal must be eaten after fasting for 12 hours and must also have at least 75 g of carbohydrates. Contrary to the normal glucose tolerance test, this test considers how the body reacts to all aspects of the food, such as starch and sugar. This test is mostly performed at home on patients diagnosed with diabetes to determine if they are getting the right amount of insulin. Therefore, we do not typically do this testing.

Tip #36: 3 Hour Glucose Testing

Three-hour glucose tolerance testing is not very enjoyable for our patients but is a necessary evil. This test is administered to patients who failed the one-hour glucose tolerance test and need to be more carefully evaluated for gestational diabetes. For this test, a patient must be fasting for at least 8 hours. When they arrive, they will get a fasting glucose drawn, which must be between 70 and 140 mg/dl. If it is outside these ranges, we consult with their provider on what their next steps should be. If the patient has had anything other than water, we must reschedule the test for a different day. After the fasting glucose is drawn, the patient drinks 100g glucola in under 5 minutes. Once the patient is finished, we write down the three draw times. These times will be 1 hour, 2 hours, and 3 hours after the time that they finished the glucola. This allows the doctor to see the rate at which their body processes the glucose more in-depth. Only water is permitted while the patient is waiting for the next draw. The test must be over if a patient vomits or has to eat something to stave off nausea. If the patient fails a 3-hour glucose tolerance test, they have to monitor their glucose level with a glucometer for the remainder of their pregnancy.

Tip #37: OB Panel

An OB Panel is something specific to our laboratory; however, it contains all of the routine tests that are performed during the first few obstetrician appointments after pregnancy is confirmed. In this panel, we draw 2 SSTs, 1 K2EDTA, and 1 EDTA, and collect a clean catch urine sample. In addition, we test for CBC w/differential, Rubella IgG, Syphilis Trep-Sure EIA, Hepatitis Bs Antigen, RBC Antibody Screen, ABO, Rho(D), HIV Ag/Ab, and a Urine Culture. In some cases, a doctor will also order a Urinalysis w/Microscopy or a Chlamydia/GC PCR Urine.

These tests are important to determine if there is anything in the mother's blood that is going to affect the pregnancy or if there is a need for the Rhogam shot. The Rhogam shot is administered to mothers that are Rh-negative (A-, O-, B-, AB-) since there can be a conflict if the mother's blood is Rh-positive (A+, O+, B+, or AB+).

Tip #38: hCG Confirmation/Hormone levels

hCG confirmation is something done when there is a high-risk pregnancy, a suspicion of a chemical pregnancy, a lower-than-expected hCG level, or to judge the timeline of a pregnancy. hCG is the human chorionic gonadotropin, which is the hormone that surges in women who are pregnant. For a woman who is not pregnant, this level should normally be under 5 mIU/mL, but in pregnant women, the number starts low and doubles each day of pregnancy. Women typically take a urine test, which will come back positive if there is higher than a level of 5 mIU/mL. During your first doctor's appointment with your OB, they will typically do a blood test to see how far along you are and compare it to the date of your last period to estimate your due date.

There are different levels of hormones in everyone's body, but typically the one tested for during pregnancy or in hopes of pregnancy is your progesterone level. Doctors may measure your progesterone level if you are having trouble getting pregnant since the results can suggest whether or not you are ovulating. Patients usually get this test drawn at either 18 or 24 days after the first day of their period. Doctors will also get progesterone drawn on their pregnant patients to check the health of the pregnancy. The doctor may order this test if there is a risk of a miscarriage or other complications.

Most Common Laboratory Panels

Tip #39: Comprehensive Metabolic Panel

A comprehensive metabolic panel (CMP) can be drawn either fasting or non-fasting, based on provider preference and the order.

A CMP is collected in either an SST or a PST and requires a minimum of 3.0mL of whole blood (2.0mL of serum). A comprehensive metabolic panel (CMP) includes:

- Sodium:

Sodium (Na) is an alkali metal element on the periodic table. Sodium helps to maintain normal blood pressure and helps regulate the fluid balances in the body. Having a low or a high sodium level can point to many different diseases and conditions and aids doctors in discovering what might be wrong with their patients. This is also extremely helpful in situations determining if a patient is overhydrated or dehydrated.

- AST (Aspartame Aminotransferase):

AST is an enzyme present in the liver. Testing the level can help diagnose liver problems.

- Bilirubin Total:

Bilirubin is a compound found in your liver that can cause a yellow-orange color change in the skin and, in great amounts, the eyes. Bilirubin is the result of blood cells breaking down and can suggest a problem with the liver. Bilirubin is secreted through stool, which is why so many newborns have higher bilirubin. Since it sometimes takes a while for their bodies to pass their first stool. Doctors monitor this level, and if they are concerned, the babies are placed under phototherapy lights until their bilirubin lowers to a normal level.

- Albumin:

Albumin is a protein made in the liver to help regulate the function of your bloodstream. Low albumin can signal a whole host of different conditions.

- Creatinine:

Creatinine is a waste product or the result of a breakdown in creatine phosphate that comes from muscle and protein metabolism. Creatinine levels can signify kidney diseases and impairments.

- Alkaline Phosphatase:

Alkaline Phosphatase (ALP) is an enzyme found throughout your body. Abnormal levels of ALP can signify problems with your bones, liver, or gallbladder.

- BUN (Blood Urea Nitrogen):

Measures the amount of nitrogen present in one's blood as a result of urea. This can help diagnose kidney problems.

- Calcium:

Calcium (Ca) is one of the most important minerals found in your body. A blood test can determine the amount of calcium present and help determine if there are any health concerns with your bones, heart, nerves, kidneys, etc.

- ALT (Alanine Transaminase):

ALT is an enzyme present in the liver. Testing this level can help diagnose liver problems.

- Potassium:

Potassium (K) is a salt necessary to help your heart and muscles work properly. Having a high potassium level can mean serious heart problems and must be taken seriously. Hemolysis of a potassium blood sample will confound results and must be redrawn.

- Chloride:

Chloride (Cl-) is a chemical compound created when chlorine gains an electron, making it negatively charged. Chloride is a type of salt.

- Glucose:

Glucose testing measures the amount of glucose in your blood and helps determine if your liver is doing an efficient job at processing your glucose intake. Glucose levels are one of the biggest indicators of diabetes.

- Protein:

A total protein blood test will show the amount of protein in your blood. Abnormal levels of protein can be an indicator of kidney or liver problems, coupled with signs and symptoms that are reported to your doctor.

- CO2:

CO2 (Carbon Dioxide) is the waste product of used oxygen. We breathe in a combination of oxygen and other trace elements and expel CO2. The CO2 level in the blood will help doctors determine if the patient's lungs are working well enough on their own to expel the CO2.

Tip #40: Basic Metabolic Panel

A Basic Metabolic Panel can be drawn either fasting or non-fasting based on provider preference and the order. It has a minimum of 2.0 mL of whole blood (1.0 mL of serum) in an SST tube for its collection. This panel includes:

- Creatinine:

Creatinine is a waste product or the result of a breakdown in creatine phosphate that comes from muscle and protein metabolism. Creatinine levels can signify kidney diseases and impairments.

- Sodium:

Sodium (Na) is an alkali metal element on the periodic table. Sodium helps to maintain normal blood pressure and helps regulate the fluid balances in the body. Having a low or a high sodium level can point to many different diseases and conditions and aids doctors in discovering what might be wrong with their patients. This is also extremely helpful in situations determining if a patient is overhydrated or dehydrated.

- BUN (Blood Urea Nitrogen):

Measures the amount of nitrogen that is present in one's blood as a result of urea. This can help diagnose kidney problems.

- Calcium:

Calcium (Ca) is one of the most important minerals found in your body. A blood test can determine the amount of calcium present and help determine if there are any health concerns with your bones, heart, nerves, kidneys, etc.

- Potassium:

Potassium (K) is a salt necessary for your heart and muscles to work properly. Having a high potassium level can mean serious heart problems and must be taken seriously. Hemolysis of a potassium blood sample will confound results and must be redrawn.

- Chloride:

Chloride (Cl-) is a chemical compound created when chlorine gains an electron, making it negatively charged. Chloride is a type of salt.

- Glucose:

Glucose testing measures the amount of glucose in your blood and helps determine if your liver is doing an efficient job at processing your glucose intake. Glucose levels are one of the most significant indicators of diabetes.

- CO2:

CO2 (Carbon Dioxide) is the waste product of used oxygen. We breathe in a combination of oxygen and other trace elements and expel CO2. CO2 in the blood will help doctors determine if the patient's lungs are working well enough on their own to expel the CO2 from their bodies.

Tip #41: Renal Function Panel

A Renal Function Panel is drawn using an SST and requires a minimum of 2.0 mL of whole blood that produces 1.0 mL of serum. This testing is not subject to a fasting requirement. A Renal Function Panel includes:

- Albumin:

Albumin is a protein made in the liver to help regulate the function of your bloodstream. Low albumin can signal a whole host of different conditions.

- BUN (Blood Urea Nitrogen):

Measures the amount of nitrogen that is present in one's blood as a result of urea. This can help diagnose kidney problems.

- Creatinine:

Creatinine is a waste product or the result of a breakdown in creatine phosphate that comes from muscle and protein metabolism. Creatinine levels can signify kidney diseases and impairments.

- Phosphorus:

Phosphorus (P) is a chemical element and is a necessary mineral in the bloodstream. Phosphorus and calcium work together to promote strong bones and teeth. Abnormal phosphorus levels can be a sign of kidney disease or other serious conditions that need to be seen by a doctor.

- Sodium:

Sodium (Na) is an alkali metal element on the periodic table. Sodium helps to maintain normal blood pressure and helps regulate the fluid balances in the body. Having a low or a high sodium level can point to many different diseases and conditions and aids doctors in discovering what might be wrong with their patients. This is also extremely helpful in situations determining if a patient is overhydrated or dehydrated.

- Potassium:

Potassium (K) is a salt necessary to help your heart and muscles work properly. Having a high potassium level can mean serious heart problems and must be taken seriously. Hemolysis of a potassium blood sample will confound results and must be redrawn.

- CO_2:

CO_2 (Carbon Dioxide) is the waste product of used oxygen. We breathe in a combination of oxygen and other trace elements and expel CO_2. CO_2 in the blood will help doctors determine if the patient's lungs are working well enough on their own to expel the CO_2 from their bodies.

- Chloride:

Chloride (Cl-) is a chemical compound created when chlorine gains an electron, making it negatively charged. Chloride is a type of salt.

- Calcium:

Calcium (Ca) is one of the most important minerals found in your body. A blood test can determine the amount of calcium present and help determine if there are any health concerns with your bones, heart, nerves, kidneys, etc.

- Glucose:

Glucose testing measures the amount of glucose in your blood and helps determine if your liver is doing an efficient job at processing your glucose intake. Glucose levels are one of the most significant indicators of diabetes.

- Osmolality Calculated:

Osmolality calculated measures concentrations of different substances in your blood, urine, and stool. This tests urea, glucose, sodium, potassium, and various other electrolytes to ensure that the liver and kidneys are working properly.

Tip #42: Lipid Panel

A Lipid Panel can be drawn either fasting or non-fasting based on provider preference and the order. It is drawn in an SST and has a minimum of 2.0 mL of whole blood for a product of 1.0mL of serum. A Lipid Panel includes:

- Triglycerides:

Triglycerides are a type of fat in your body that can contribute to heart diseases and liver diseases. High triglyceride levels can lead to the hardening of the arteries with plaque that leads to your heart.

- Cholesterol:

Cholesterol comes in two forms, HDL and LDL. This test computes the total cholesterol present in the blood and can determine your risk for heart problems. It can also help to determine genetic problems.

- HDL (High-Density Lipoprotein):

High-Density Lipoprotein is good cholesterol since it carries cholesterol back to the liver and allows your liver to process and get rid of the cholesterol in your body.

- Calculations for LDL (Low-Density Lipoprotein):

Low-Density Lipoprotein is bad cholesterol since it does not transport down to the liver but rather causes a build-up in your arteries and can lead to severe heart conditions and heart attacks. This number is found by taking the total cholesterol number and subtracting the number of HDL found in your body.

- Calculations for Total/HDL Cholesterol Ratio:

This is measured by dividing your total cholesterol number (found in the testing) by the level of HDL found in your blood. These numbers can provide the doctor with answers about your heart health.

Tip #43: Thyroid Function Panel

A Thyroid Function Panel (Also called a Thyroid Profile) is drawn in an SST with a minimum requirement of 1.0 mL of whole blood of 0.5mL of serum. This testing is not subject to a fasting requirement. This testing is not performed often. Most often, doctors order a TSH with reflex to Free T4, or they will order them separately. A Thyroid Function panel includes:

- Free T4 (Thyroxine):

Thyroxine is the main hormone that is secreted by the thyroid gland. This test is performed if you are exhibiting symptoms of an overactive or underactive thyroid. These tests can come back as abnormal if you have abnormal estrogen levels or are pregnant. An overactive thyroid can be a symptom of many different diseases.

- TSH (Thyroid Stimulating Hormone):

Thyroid Stimulating Hormone is secreted by your pituitary gland that promotes your thyroid gland to secrete thyroxine. This is why providers sometimes test your TSH before testing your free T4. The thyroid is extremely important for secreting hormones that are necessary for the body to behave normally, and blood tests to test its function are drawn very frequently.

Tip #44: Liver Function Panel

A Liver Function Panel is drawn in an SST with a minimum of 2.0 mL of whole blood, resulting in 1.0 mL of serum. This testing is not subject to a fasting requirement. A Liver Function Panel includes:

- AST (Aspartame Aminotransferase):

AST is an enzyme present in the liver. Testing the level can help diagnose liver problems

- Bilirubin (Total):

Total bilirubin measures the bilirubin in the blood to see how well the liver is working and if it is filtering the way it should be. If this number is high, it indicates something may be wrong with the liver or intestinal tract.

- Bilirubin (Direct):

Direct bilirubin is also drawn if the TC bili is higher than 14 and can be tested using the same blood sample from the total bilirubin. A direct bilirubin tests for a blockage in the bile ducts in either the liver or the gallbladder.

- Albumin:

Albumin is a protein made in the liver to help regulate the function of your bloodstream. Low albumin can signal a whole host of different conditions.

- Protein:

A total protein blood test will show the amount of protein in your blood. Abnormal levels of protein can be an indicator of kidney or liver problems, coupled with signs and symptoms that are reported to your doctor.

- ALT(Alanine Transaminase):

ALT is an enzyme present in the liver. Testing this level can help diagnose liver problems.

- Alkaline Phosphatase:

Alkaline Phosphatase (ALP) is an enzyme found throughout your body. Abnormal levels of ALP can signify problems with your bones, liver, or gallbladder.

Tip #45: Electrolyte Panel

An Electrolyte Panel is drawn in an SST with a minimum of 2.0 mL of whole blood, resulting in 1.0 mL of serum. This testing is not subject to a fasting requirement. An Electrolyte Panel includes:

- Sodium:

Sodium (Na) is an alkali metal element on the periodic table. Sodium helps to maintain normal blood pressure and helps regulate the fluid balances in the body. Having a low or a high sodium level can point to many different diseases and conditions and aids doctors in discovering what might be wrong with their patients. This is also extremely helpful in situations determining if a patient is overhydrated or dehydrated.

- Potassium:

Potassium (K) is a salt necessary to help your heart and muscles work properly. Having a high potassium level can mean serious heart problems and must be taken seriously. Hemolysis of a potassium blood sample will confound results and must be redrawn.

- Chloride:

Chloride (Cl-) is a chemical compound created when chlorine gains an electron, making it negatively charged. Chloride is a type of salt.

- CO_2:

CO_2 (Carbon Dioxide) is the waste product of used oxygen. We breathe in a combination of oxygen and other trace elements and expel CO_2. CO_2 in the blood will help doctors determine if the patient's lungs are working well enough on their own to expel the CO_2 from their bodies.

Tip #46: Allergy Panel

Allergy Panels are panels constructed by doctors that include allergy tests that a patient suspects that they may be allergic to. Blood allergy tests yield a false positive 50-60% of the time and are rarely conducted. Each of the following tests is performed in an

SST, and all require less than 1 mL of blood for each. The following is a list of allergy blood tests that we offer:

- Allergen, Drugs, Penicillin G (major)
- Allergen, Drugs, Penicillin V (minor)
- Allergen, Food, Avocado
- Allergen, Food, Baker's Yeast/Brewer's Yeast
- Allergen, Food, Barley
- Allergen, Food, Hops
- Allergen, Food, Pepper C. frutescens IgE
- Allergen, Food, Pork
- Allergen, Food, Red Dye/Carmine (Red 4) IgE
- Allergen, Food, Rye
- Allergen, Food, Tuna
- Allergen, Grass, Alfalfa IgE
- Allergen, Grass, Cultivated Corn Pollen
- Allergen, Tree, Cedar/Red Tree
- Allergen, Tree, White Ash Tree
- Allergen, Weed, Giant Ragweed
- Allergens, Animal, Dog/Cat Epithelium Profile

Tip #47: Complete Blood Count w/differential

A complete blood count usually includes differential, which is further testing for anemia and other blood conditions and infections. If your doctor is not concerned about these things, they may order a complete blood count without differential. Typically, I draw CBCs with differential. CBCs are drawn in whole blood purple top EDTA tubes. 4.0 mL is the preferred specimen, but 1.0mL is also accepted as a minimum typically. A Complete Blood Count w/differential (CBC w/diff) includes:

- Red Blood Cell Count (RBC):

Red blood cells transport oxygen throughout the body. Red blood cells are produced by bone marrow and contain hemoglobin. RBC can help to diagnose heart diseases and anemia.

- White Blood Cell Count (WBC):

White blood cells work to fight infections and heal the body. A low white cell count can mean that the body is unable to protect itself from diseases, and the patient may be immunocompromised. Alternatively, if the white cell count is high, it can be a sign of inflammation, infections, or injury to the body. If a patient's white cell count is higher than normal and a patient is exhibiting other symptoms, many doctors order blood cultures to test for infection-causing bacteria.

- Platelet Level (PLT):

Platelets are cells that help your blood clot when it is meant to. Too low of platelets can be an indication of an infection or even some cancers. Having too many platelets makes your body clot more than it is supposed to and puts you at risk of getting clots, which could even result in strokes.

- Hemoglobin:

Hemoglobin is a protein that carries oxygen to the tissues within the body. Hemoglobin levels can indicate if a patient has internal bleeding or anemia since it signals the amount of blood we have filling our tissues. Any patient with a hemoglobin under 6 g/dL is required to get a blood transfusion. Requirements change if the patient has recurring illnesses or diagnoses.

- Hematocrit:

Hematocrit measures the level of red blood cells in your blood. If this measure is low, it can suggest anemia or low iron levels in the blood. Too high of a hematocrit can be a sign of blood diseases.

Tip #48: TC Bilirubin, Total Bilirubin, Direct Bilirubin

Transcutaneous bilirubin (TC bili) is performed on every child before they leave the hospital to detect if they have an excess of bilirubin which is extremely common. Total and direct bilirubin (a blood test off of a heel stick) is then required if a neonate has a TC bili that is above 14 within 24 hours of birth. These tests are performed as follows:

- TC bilirubin:

A TC bili is taken by an instrument called a bili meter. After scanning the newborn's patient ankle band and then your hospital ID, you take multiple scans across the baby's head in a dark room. This number must result in under 14 mg/dl.

- Total Bilirubin:

Total bilirubin is drawn if the TC bili is higher than 14, and it is done by taking blood from the heel of an infant. Six hundred microliters must be collected in a capillary SST for this test to be run. Total bilirubin measures the bilirubin in the blood to see how well the liver is working and if it is filtering the way it should be. If this number is high, it indicates something may be wrong with the liver or intestinal tract.

- Direct Bilirubin:

Direct bilirubin is also drawn if the TC bili is higher than 14 and can be tested using the same blood sample from the total bilirubin. A direct bilirubin tests for a blockage in the bile ducts in either the liver or the gallbladder.

Chapter Review

- While glucose tolerance tests, just like all other laboratory tests, are not forced on you, they are extremely important for your pregnancy. It is not fun or comfortable, but it allows your provider to provide specific care for you and your baby. Having untreated gestational diabetes can cause major problems for your unborn baby, such as premature birth, stillbirth, excessive birth weight, and serious breathing difficulties. Therefore, even if you are late to care, you should still get this testing performed.
- Allergy panels are not covered by insurance unless there are specific allergies that are affecting a patient that must be tested for. Therefore, it is unlikely that insurance would pay for a complete allergen panel with no cause or suspicion of allergens other than curiosity. That being said, allergen blood tests are extremely helpful to parents of young children when they are reacting to something and can't pinpoint what it is.
- Neonate bilirubin transcutaneous testing is required by most hospitals before a newborn is discharged. If there is a requirement for blood collection, there is a grey area. Some religions do not allow for blood collection, or some parents do not allow it. That being said, there is mandatory newborn screening that is performed to test for serious conditions. This is also a blood test, and the parents will most times be reported to child services if they do not allow this testing to occur without a religious exemption. You have to advocate for your child, so you can always say no to certain phlebotomists and only allow certain people to draw your child. If the phlebotomist takes more than 5 minutes to draw the blood after sticking your child's heel, it is too long. You can always ask questions and voice your concerns. If you are nervous about anything, ask your nurse to be in the room when the draw occurs.
- A complete metabolic panel is more in-depth than a basic metabolic panel. A provider may order a BMP if they are more concerned about an electrolyte or fluid problem rather

than kidney and liver functions. A BMP is also recommended for a general metabolism overview rather than performing extensive tests that have no use at the time. A CMP will be used when doctors are unsure of why symptoms are arising or if they have specific concerns regarding the liver.

- OB testing usually occurs between 8 and 12 weeks but can occur later if a patient doesn't know about the pregnancy or chooses not to come in for care. OB testing is extremely important because certain diseases such as HIV and Syphilis require special care during pregnancy. If a patient has a vaginal infection near the time of delivery, it could cause complications, or a doctor might suggest a Cesarean section instead. HIV in babies can cause complications and adverse reactions after birth and should be carefully supervised during and after the pregnancy.

Chapter 4: Emergency Room/Atypical Labs and Occurrences

Key terms in this chapter: Syringes, Legality, Trauma, STAT, and Protocols.

Uncommon Testing

Tip #49: iSTATs

iSTATs are handheld devices used to run blood work in under two minutes at a patient's bedside. They are about a foot long, five inches wide, and either blue and white or white and grey. There is a scanner located at the top of the iSTAT used to scan your hospital badge, the patient's wrist band, and the cartridge that you are using. There is an opening at the bottom of the iSTAT on the opposite side of the scanner, where you plug the cartridge in once it is filled with blood. Finally, there is a small screen on the front of the iSTAT that will give you step-by-step instructions.

To fill an iSTAT cartridge, you will need a syringe with blood or a glass capillary tube. Place the end of the syringe above the circle on the bottom right-hand side of the cartridge and slowly deposit a drop of blood. The blood will move up the tubing above the circle. Continue giving a drop of blood at a time until it is ¾ full. Carefully–without touching anything besides the edges of the cartridge–close the stopper over the circle opening; this should push the blood the remainder of the way up. If you are using a glass capillary tube, place the blood side flush to the iSTAT opening and release your finger from the opposite side. This will release the blood into the opening and fill the cartridge. Close the stopper and insert it into the iSTAT. Sometimes the process can create a mess on the outside of the cartridge, so do your best to wipe away excess blood with an alcohol swab after the stopper is secured over the opening.

The iSTAT unit comes with a separate printer with a screen as well. The screen of the printer must be matched up with the scanner of the iSTAT to print out the results of the blood work on a little receipt-sized paper for the doctors. iSTATs are always run on stroke alert patients and trauma patients with Chem8+ cartridges. These cartridges test the patient's chemistries, glucose, blood gas, etc. They are used for expedited testing in cases of emergencies.

We can run different cartridges on the iSTATs for the different tests that are needed. For example, if I have a patient who is possibly having a stroke, I would run a Chem8+ cartridge on them. The other cartridges I can use are 6+, Crea, G, EC4+, CG8+, and E3+. The hospital I worked at had POC glucometers, so we didn't have to use the G cartridge. We also typically never used any other cartridge than the Chem8+.

CG8+ cartridges are extremely helpful for venous blood gases since they result quickly and are as accurate as laboratory testing. Another test we perform with iSTATs is routine creatinine testing before a patient gets an MRI as an outpatient.

Tip #50: Blood Alcohol Content Testing

Blood alcohol content testing can go one of two ways—either the patient will comply or they will not. If the patient complies, everything goes well, and it will take you ten minutes. If the patient does not comply, the officer and a nurse will restrain the patient while you are taking the blood. It may be uncomfortable, but once a warrant is served, it is no longer up to the patient whether or not to get drawn.

Blood alcohol testing occurs when a person refuses a breathalyzer test or has to be admitted to the hospital in custody and is believed to be under the influence. Before drawing the patient's blood, the police officer will need an active warrant for specimen collection. This warrant acts just like a warrant would if a police officer were taking custody of your purse. When you arrive at the Emergency

Department (ED), you will need to get a BAC kit that will include a cardboard box, a plastic container with foam, an iodine swab (you cannot use alcohol since it will confound the results), a needle with a hub, a tube, a form, and seals. You will sign the form, the officer will sign the form, and the charge nurse will sign the form. The officer and the charge nurse must be in the room and watch you draw the patient sample. Next, you will label the tube, place the tube and the covered needle into the box with foam, seal the plastic box with the given do-not-break police seals, and initial all of the spaces where the seal meets the box. Next, you place the small box that contains the needle and the tube into the bigger cardboard box. Then seal the cardboard box with the do-not-break police seals and initial everywhere the seal touches the box. Then the police officer will also initial at all the seals on the box. Finally, the officer will also fill out the top of the box in accordance with their policies to identify the patient and case number.

Specific Patient Types

Tip #51: Drawing a Suicidal Patient

I want to take this opportunity to talk about suicide. If you or anyone that you know is having suicidal thoughts, please call the National Suicide Prevention Hotline at:

800-283-8255

Even if you don't have plans, even if it is just an entertaining thought, take the time to give them a call. I have seen so many families ripped apart when their loved ones have taken their lives, and it is never worth it. If you are in high school, talk to a favorite teacher or counselor. If you're an adult, find a support group nearby or call a friend or a sibling. I promise that someone would rather be woken up at three in the morning with a call from you rather than the police.

In some cases, patients will try to refuse to get their blood drawn after attempting suicide. At this point, the doctor has assumed responsibility for the patient, or a power of attorney for the patient has that responsibility. The patient no longer has to capacity to make logical decisions for themselves. If they still refuse, the police officer who is stationed in their room along with their nurse will help hold down the patient while you draw their blood.

Overdoses:

When a person attempts suicide in any way, they should be taken to the hospital. If the emergency room determines they have no physical ailments, they will be moved to mental health triage. If they have taken pills or overdosed orally, they will either have their stomach pumped or be given a charcoal drink. The activated charcoal in the drink prevents the poison or medication from being absorbed from the stomach and into the rest of the body. If a patient overdoses on an intravenous drug, they will be given Narcan by emergency services before getting to the hospital. If a patient overdoses on alcohol and gets alcohol poisoning, they should be taken to the hospital. Even if it was accidental, alcohol acts as a depressant, and in extremely large quantities, it can suppress the respiratory and circulatory systems and cause organ failure and death.

Even in a nonemergent case of alcohol poisoning, patients can be belligerent and dangerous or could pass out and asphyxiate on their own vomit. Overdose patients are at a high risk of seizures due to ingesting or injecting so many drugs, so watch for the signs that a seizure is about to begin. Different blood tests are ordered depending on if the patient reported what they took or if the doctors don't know.

Other Methods:

If you are drawing a suicidal patient that has sliced their wrists vertically, you can still draw from their antecubital vein. Depending on the amount of blood that was lost, it may be more difficult than normal. If a patient has attempted to drown themselves, their veins may also be more rigid and less prevalent due to a low temperature. Each different method of suicide comes with its own difficulties. Always treat your patients with kindness and respect. The nurse will have them restrained or sedated if they are violent or reactive. If you ever feel uncomfortable, you can always ask a nurse to accompany you to the room. There will be a variety of different blood work ordered, but if blood is lost, there will always be hemoglobin or a CBC ordered.

Tip #52: Drawing a Trauma Patient

At the hospital where I worked, traumas would be announced over the PA system. For example, "Trauma incoming by air five minutes, ED room 14". This signifies that there is a trauma being flown in, and they will arrive on the roof in five minutes and be transported to ED room 14 for assessment. If the announcement said, "Trauma incoming by ground ten minutes, ED room 14", it would mean a trauma is coming in by ambulance, and they will arrive in the ambulance bay in ten minutes, and the patient will be transported to ED room 14. The hospital operators know this information from the ambulance drivers radioing in and announcing their distance and the patient information. When trauma alerts go off, you stop what you are doing or finish the draw that you are on and go down to the emergency department. Most times, you will arrive before they do. At that time, get your tubes ready. The computer won't have any orders or any patient information since the patient might not have been identified yet.

You are going to draw a rainbow—Sodium Citrate, Lithium Heparin, Plasma Separator, Serum Separator, K2EDTA (or Blood

Bank), EDTA, and run an iSTAT Chem8+. There will be about 20 people in the trauma room, and it will be the calm before the storm.

The paramedics will bring the patient in on a stretcher and start reading off their stats in the ambulance, what happened to the patient, and any health information that they know. The paramedics and firefighters will sit outside the room and wait as the nurses transfer the patient from the stretcher to the table. The nurses will then take a pair of scissors and cut the patient's clothing off—shirt, bra, pants, underwear, and any other garments. A nurse will start an IV on the patient, and you will hand them two 20 mL syringes for the blood you need. If they are struggling and the doctors instruct you to attempt to draw blood, then you will start looking for a vein. Wait for the doctors, respiratory therapists, and nurses to do their initial workup before going in for blood work.

There will often be X-rays taken, and the technician will announce them before taking them. Most medical personnel will clear the room at this point if they aren't currently treating the patient. After you get your 40mL of blood, use a transfer device to fill the iSTAT first and get it running, then fill all of your tubes. Once the stat is finished, give the results to the charge nurse, and they will relay them to the doctor when it is appropriate. Sometimes these situations are very bloody and gory, but you must maintain professionalism the entire time. If you need to leave the room, try to finish your task first but, if necessary, take a step out. The doctors are doing the best that they can. There have been times when I have drawn a trauma patient who didn't look too injured, but I hear on the news the next day that they didn't make it. There have been times when I have wanted to pass out when the stretcher is pulled out from under them and blood splats onto the floor. There have even been times when I go up on the floor to draw patients, see them in the ICU, and feel a little bit anxious all over again. I just always say to myself that everyone is doing their best for the patient and that these things can happen to anyone. Even if a patient is unconscious or brain dead, I personally still talk to them like they are awake, "Alright, now this is going to be just a quick poke." Just in case they can hear me, it also makes me feel better about drawing them.

Tip #53: Drawing a Stroke Patient

Strokes occur when a blood clot travels to the brain. During a stroke alert at the hospital where I worked, the PA system would announce "Stroke alert ED room 10" and would require you to get to that room within five minutes. They will also announce stroke alerts on the patient floors. If you arrive at an alert and the patient's bed is gone, they most likely have taken your patient for their scan. Ask the nurse how long it will be; if it will be under 10 minutes and you do not have any more draws, wait for them to return.

There are a lot of signs and symptoms that can suggest a stroke, and a CT scan can confirm it. The CT scan will also show if you have suffered from an ischemic stroke or a hemorrhagic stroke. An MRI can also show a stroke, but CTs are often used because they are quicker and allow the patient to get sufficient treatment as soon as possible. For a stroke alert, you will draw a Chem8+ iSTAT as well as a rainbow if there are no orders in for the patient. If there are orders in for the patient, then draw them accordingly. If the orders are not in the computer, you will need to label the tubes with patient labels found in the patient chart. You cannot, under any circumstances, send samples down to the laboratory without labels; they will be rejected.

Tip #54: Drawing a Sepsis Patient

Sepsis occurs when you have an infection, and when your body tries to fight the infection, it causes inflammation. This can cause damage to a multitude of organs and even cause them to shut down. During a sepsis alert at the hospital where I worked, the PA system would announce "Sepsis alert ED room 12". This alert means that a patient who is already in the ED is showing signs of sepsis, and doctors need to complete testing rapidly. There will also be sepsis alerts on the patient floors, especially in the ICU. If this occurs, you still need to get to the room as soon as possible. Sepsis rooms have contact precautions due to the patient having an unknown infection. You are to wear a plastic tear-away gown over your lab coat and wear gloves and eye protection. If there are no orders in for the patient, you draw a rainbow and two sets of cultures. Draw the patient for one set of cultures and also draw the rainbow off of that spot. Attempt for the second set of cultures if possible. If there are already orders entered, draw the orders accordingly. Once they enter these orders into the computer, they are time-coded and almost always marked as STAT. STAT orders need to be drawn within 15 minutes of the time they are ordered.

Chapter Review

- iSTAT machines are extremely valuable equipment available to medical personnel to use when there is no time to wait for traditional blood work to be run in a lab. Be sure that your cartridges are not expired prior to use and that you are selecting the correct cartridge for the testing needed.
- Never do a BAC test alone if you do not know what you are doing, and never draw the patient until the nurse manager and the arresting officer is in the room to observe.
- Treat suicidal patients with the care and decency you would want if you were in that situation. If they are refusing a lab draw, have the doctor speak to them about their inability to make decisions for themselves.
- When drawing a trauma patient, be sure to draw an entire rainbow so the blood will be available for the lab when the doctor finally enters the orders.
- Stroke and sepsis patients occur both in the ED and on the patient floors. Both should be handled with urgency and responded to as soon as possible.
- If orders for trauma, stroke, or sepsis patients are not in the computer, draw what the protocol calls for (trauma-rainbow, stroke-rainbow + iSTAT Chem8+, sepsis- rainbow +2 sets of blood cultures) and label with patient labels. Never send unlabeled specimens down to the lab; they will be thrown away.

Chapter 5: Plasma Collections Phlebotomy

Key terms in this chapter: Tubing, Pressure, Tension, Allergies, Adjustments, and Misses.

Phlebotomist Errors

Tip #55: Hematomas, Bruises, Infiltrations, and Blown Veins

Hematomas are bruises that are severe enough that the blood pooling around the vein makes a visible bump or bubble. If one were to take a syringe to this bubble, there would be blood. In plasma donations, hematomas occur when the needle blows a vein or infiltrates a vein and causes the blood or saline to be returned into the arms tissue instead. The machine will catch this mistake as the pressure will be significantly higher than it should be, and it will alarm. Most times, however, your patient will be the first to alarm you since there will be a lot of pain concentrated around the venipuncture site. Hematomas can be as small as a marble or as large as a golf ball and will present either without discoloration or with growing discoloration. If it is just an infiltration, the discoloration will occur slowly as the blood seeps out of the vein and into the surrounding areas. The discoloration will be immediate and more painful if it is a blown vein.

Bruises occur when blood seeps into the tissue near the surface of the skin. For example, if I bump into a table and my thigh is bruised, it's because my capillaries burst from the impact, and it left a mark that gets progressively worse and then better. As bruises heal, you may see them begin as dark blue or purple and turn lighter into yellow or green. This has to do with the hemoglobin breakdown in the blood. When you burst your capillaries, it releases blood that needs to be reabsorbed. The discoloration will get lighter as the blood becomes less pooled and more spread out. Blood is naturally blue under the skin until it is exposed to oxygen, and then it turns red. This is why bruises begin as a bluish hue and are the darkest within a couple of days of the injury.

Infiltrations occur often and are either very problematic or unproblematic. As a phlebotomist, I want to inflict as minimal pain as possible on my patient, but sometimes it's unavoidable. If I am doing a simple lab draw from a vein that will not be used again anytime soon, it does not create a major problem to accidentally infiltrating the vein. If I am adjusting my needle and it pierces through to the other side of the vein, it will be uncomfortable for the patient, but it may still allow me to draw blood from the vein. Infiltrations during a blood draw usually only produce minimal bruises. Infiltrations during plasma donation are a different story. Imagine you are holding a juice pouch. There is one hole where the juice is supposed to come out, and the juice will come out slowly if you remove the straw. If you accidentally pierce through the other side of the juice box with the straw, the juice will also start spilling out of the other side. But, if you start to pour more juice into the juice box with the hole on the other side, the juice box leaks faster and gets larger than it is meant to be. This is how it is if we try to return saline or blood cells to a patient who has an infiltrated vein. The return will not just go back into the vein but will leave more aggressively out of the other side of the vein and fill the available space with fluid rather than having it go back into the vein as it should. Neither one is particularly harmful to the patient, but there will be a lot of pressure and stinging occurring.

Blown veins are the phlebotomist lingo for severe infiltration or a collapsed vein. Normal infiltrations will allow the blood to leak out slowly from both holes in the vein. Severe infiltrations that we call blown veins are veins that immediately appear as a bruise as soon as the infiltration occurs. This is a lot more painful for the patient as the pressure is immediate and intense. In addition, you can see as the blood seeps out into the surrounding areas. This can occur when the needle is just too big for a vein to handle or the speed at which fluid is going into the vein is too high. Collapsed veins are infiltrated veins that cave in and cut off the blood flow for the vein. It is not harmful to the patient other than the painful sensation. The vein will heal itself in a few weeks. You can tell when a vein has collapsed when you feel a strong vein, and after venipuncture, the vein disappears. Or you get a flash or a small amount of blood, but it won't flow again no matter how much you adjust.

Tip #56: Clotting and Hemolysis

Clotting occurs naturally when blood is exposed to air—the proteins in your blood, along with the platelets to stop the bleeding. As a phlebotomist, your goal is to collect a sufficient specimen for laboratory testing. For tubes such as PST, SST, and Red Top-clotting is the goal. For tubes such as EDTA or K2EDTA, there should be no clotting. If clotting occurs in an EDTA venous tube or a capillary tube, the sample will be discarded and needs to be redrawn. The biggest problem surrounding clotting is pediatric capillary draws. When a neonate or a young child needs a capillary draw for an EDTA, you only have a small window of time to get the blood from their finger and into the tube once you start. If you take too long to invert the tube and mix in the EDTA, the sample will clot, and you'll need to recollect. This is rarely an issue with heel pokes, but rather with finger sticks on young kids. It makes it extremely difficult when they have little fingers that clamp up the second you poke their finger. The blood will get everywhere for just one drop, and it takes quite some time to get enough blood for a sample, presenting an opportunity for clotting.

Hemolysis is when the red blood cells in a sample are damaged or destroyed. This happens most frequently with capillary draws with the intensity of the squeezing, but not always. When we use smaller needles such as a 25 gauge or when we need to move the needle around excessively, adjusting the needle can damage the blood cells during a collection as it jostles the vein around. Testing cannot be performed accurately on hemolyzed blood since it can record inaccurate levels of electrolytes in the blood. It is better just to do the first stick well than to try and risk it and have to come back and draw again later. Potassium is an electrolyte that can be very telling when looking for heart problems. If it is elevated or lower than normal, it will affect the medications the patient is prescribed. For example, potassium of 5 can result in as high as 7.6 if the sample is extremely hemolyzed.

Setting up Patients for Plasma Collections

Tip #57: Aurora Machines

Aurora machines are the pumps we attach plastic tubing onto and connect to the patient for plasma collection. When preparing an aurora machine, we carefully put the plastic tubing on so that it will not get caught and shredded in the pumps. On these machines, there is an outline of how the tubing goes in, but after a week or so, it becomes muscle memory. There are four ends to the tubing—one that is hooked up to the anticoagulant, one that is hooked up to the saline, one that will hook onto the butterfly needle, and one that is hooking up to the collection bottle. In each patient kit, there is:

- A tubing set up
- A bag of anticoagulant
- A bag of saline
- An 18-gauge butterfly needle
- A collection bottle
- An iodine swab

When setting up a patient in a center, you have a handheld module or paper that you verify a patient's first name, last name, date of birth, and the last four of the social security number. This verifies the person's identity. The module will then prompt you to scan the barcodes on the items you are using to make sure that they have the correct lot numbers. After this step, you will put the setup onto the machine, press a button on it, and run air through the tubing to make sure it is all in the correct place and that there are no holes present. After confirming that the tubing is correct, the machine will prompt you to place the empty collection bottle on the bottom of the machine but closed off with a stat. Then you are prompted to spike the saline and anticoagulant bags.

Spiking is when the sharp end pieces of the tubing are thrust through the thin plastic layer on the fluid bags. Next, press the button on the machine again to run the fluid through the tubing and wait for it to give you the all-clear. Once this is done, attach the bottom end of the tubing to the bottle and take the stats off both sides.

Stats are clamps that look somewhat like scissors and are what we use to block off the tubing without perforating it. At this point, use the blood pressure cuff to act as a tourniquet to find a vein in your patient. Take the needle out of the packaging and attach a stat to the end of it so that there is a flash, but blood does not flow out the end of it.

Your module will instruct you to scrub the patient's venipuncture site with iodine in a slow circle the size of a quarter for a total of 30 seconds; once the 30 seconds is over, scrub outwards in a circle until the circle is the size of your palm. Then the module will count down 30 seconds for you to let it dry. Once the iodine is dry, inflate the blood pressure cuff again and stick the patient with the butterfly needle. Once you have a flash, secure the needle tubing with two pieces of tape an inch below the end of the needle and two pieces of tape three inches away from the bottom of the tubing for the needle.

Attach the tubing on the machine to the end of the butterfly tube and release the stats.

At this time, you will see the blood slightly advance into the tube. After this, press the start collection button on the screen of the Aurora machine and watch as the blood fills the tubing and plasma starts to drip into the collection bottle. It is important to stay next to your donor for this part to make sure there is not a kink in the tubing, a problem with the stick, a problem with the plasma, or anything else. Once the machine starts to pull blood from the donor, the blood pressure in their vein will be reported on their screen.

The machine will stop pulling blood and alarm if the needle is against a vein wall, protruding through it, or not in a vein. The machine will also alarm and stop if the color of the plasma is cloudy or red, which means lipemic plasma or the machine is depositing red cells into their plasma. Depending on how severe the coloring is, it will result in the donor either finishing the donation or being cut off.

The module will tell you, based on patient weight, how much they will be donating. Below 149 pounds, you donate 690mL of plasma; between 150-174 pounds, you donate 825mL of plasma; and at 175 pounds and above, you donate 880mL of plasma. These values are based on what is healthy and safe for us to take from our donors. All of the red cells are returned back to the donor by the end of their donation. If a donor for any reason is not able to get all of the blood returned to them, they are given a Gatorade that they need to drink and wait 15 minutes before leaving. If this happens twice within 80 days, they are suspended from donating for 80 days starting at the second occurrence. This is because the total red cell loss amounts to a whole blood donation, and those are only allowed once every 80 days for health reasons. If a patient just does not receive their saline infusion but still receives all of their red blood cells, they are not penalized any days and just need to complete the 15-minute wait and drink a Gatorade.

Tip #58: Hemoglobin and Hematocrit Importance

Each time before you donate plasma or blood, there will be a technician who will check your hematocrit or hemoglobin. It is company-specific, which one they check. At the plasma center where I worked, we checked hematocrit, but the American Red Cross checks the hemoglobin level before blood donation. Both are done by cleansing the end of a donor's finger and then piercing their skin with a lancet. Then they will wipe away the first drop of blood with gauze and then collect the blood sample with a glass capillary tube.

For hematocrit, the technician will spin the tube in a mini centrifuge. After this, they will push air into the tube so that a drop of blood goes into the hematocrit reader. Your hematocrit needs to be at least 38% for females and 40% for men to donate plasma. Hematocrit is measuring the number of red cells in your blood, and having a level lower than the recommended 38% can lead to donors passing out during donations are having adverse effects.

For hemoglobin, the blood donor technician will push a drop of your blood out onto a strip in a handheld reader. Their cut-off is having a minimum of 12.5 g/DL for females and 13.0 g/DL for males.

If your hemoglobin or hematocrit is lower than these given values, the center or blood bank will mark you as not eligible to donate. For plasma donations, you can try again the next day. For blood donations, they ask you to wait around four weeks. For women, hemoglobin and hematocrit are significantly lower during your menstrual period due to constant blood loss. To combat this, ensure you are eating enough food and drinking enough water before your donations.

Tip #59: Iodine/Alcohol/Chloraprep/Soap & Water

In my line of work, there are always different methods of cleansing. Soap and water, Alcohol swabs, Iodine, and Chloraprep, are the ones that I have used. Soap and water are used on people who are doing a blood alcohol content test or a test that you cannot use alcohol swabs on with a patient who is allergic to iodine. It is not the safest or the most effective method, but it gets the job done. Other times I use soap and water are for trace element testing on toddlers. I have them wash their entire hands since they are going to pull away from me when I'm collecting my capillary specimen. This is to make sure that I am not leaving any microscopic particles that could contain the trace elements that I am testing for.

Alcohol swabs are what is used throughout the entire medical field. They kill 99% of the bacteria that is present on the skin to prevent harmful bacteria from getting transferred from the skin to the bloodstream by the needle being inserted. You should always swab your patients for 10 seconds or more, and if the alcohol wipe comes away noticeably dirty, get another alcohol wipe to be sure that the area is clean. In addition, if at any time the patient bends their arm, touches their arm, blows on their arm, or even wafts the alcohol, you have to rescrub the area. All these activities can transfer bacteria back to the surface we just prepared.

Chloraprep is an antiseptic swab that we use when drawing blood cultures and nurses use when they are starting IVs. They are more effective than alcohol swabs because they contain an extra ingredient called CHG. However, this product still contains around 70% alcohol, so it is not appropriate to use during blood alcohol draws.

Iodine is used primarily during plasma donations because it has high antimicrobial properties that work extremely fast to kill microorganisms that may live on skin, bacteria, viruses, and nucleotides. Iodine is substituted for chloraprep during blood donations only when a donor reports that they are allergic to iodine. Iodine is not typically used in hospitals other than for disinfecting blood culture bottles before collection. Doctors and nurses use betadine for very invasive procedures such as catheters, surgeries, and any time they puncture the skin for a long period of time with a high risk of infection.

Tip #60: Scar Tissue

Scar tissue occurs in phlebotomy when a person is repeatedly stuck in the same spot. When the skin heals over the venipuncture site, there is a collection of collagen and skin cells layer on top of each other. When it occurs on a venipuncture site, it makes the skin harder to puncture. It can have a variety of different presentations. For example, it can look like a deep hole or look like a severe tightening of the skin. When you palpate someone's arm looking for a vein, it should feel smooth, bouncy, or tough. You can tell that there is scar tissue under the skin when it feels like they have a small marble in their arm. Depending on how tough this area feels, it is sometimes best to poke right above the scar tissue. If you attempt to poke through the scar tissue, you may cause unnecessary pain to the patient or damage the pain. Something that we have to deal with is "getting stuck in the scar tissue," which is when no matter how you move the needle, you can't get past the scar and into the vein. When this happens during a plasma donation stick, no blood will come out, and the machine will register a very high pressure. When this occurs during a routine blood draw, you can tell the patient that you are stuck in their scar tissue and ask them if they would like you to continue trying to adjust it or try in a different vein. Most times, I get asked just to try the other arm rather than fishing around. Scar tissue can also occur after surgeries or broken bones, but that is not my area of expertise.

Tip #61: Blood Loss and Lipemic Plasma

I mentioned blood loss earlier in regard to the amount of blood that can be lost during plasma collection and whether or not it disqualifies you from donating again. There are many ways that blood loss can occur during plasma donation. For example, if there is something wrong with the setup or the machine, the plasma could drop red, which means that the machine or the setup is allowing shredded red blood cells to be transported into the plasma. Another way that a donor can lose blood during plasma collection is by a hematoma forming in their arm and not all of their blood being able to be returned. There is also the rare occurrence that the machine tubing rips open or comes apart during donation. In the event that the line drops red or there is a hematoma, we can estimate the amount of blood lost by the donor. They can donate again the following week if this amount is low enough. In the event that the machine breaks the tubing open, we are not able to estimate how much blood has been lost, and the donor will be disqualified from donating for eight weeks.

Lipemic plasma is a cloudy-looking plasma that has fat cells present in it. When the plasma starts separating from the red cells, you will be able to see the difference. Once it passes the sensor, the machine will alarm that the plasma is an abnormal color. This occurs when a plasma donor consumes lots of fat in their diet the day before or the hours before plasma collection. While this may sound easy to avoid, some people naturally process fats slower. One person can eat a bucket of fried chicken and have perfectly clear plasma.

In comparison, another may eat just a small amount of avocado on sushi and have their plasma come back cloudy. The machine will alert when the plasma is too dark, and the plasma processors in the lab will make the decision about whether or not to end the donation. If the donation is ended, the donor is compensated for the amount of plasma they gave. If they didn't give any, they are given ten dollars compensation. If the plasma processor allows them to finish donating, they are counseled on eating fats before donation and paid in full. The term lipemic plasma comes from the word lipid. Lipids are a type of fat that have one water-loving head and two water-hating tails. Lipemic plasma results from an abundance of lipoproteins found in the blood. This often occurs after a fat-heavy meal that increases the level of triglycerides in the blood.

Tip #62: Plasma Collections Procedures

There are certain times when donors are not allowed to donate or get blacklisted from donating permanently. This can be for behavioral reasons or medical reasons. Below is a shortlist of some of the reasons that someone cannot donate or causes for being blacklisted:

- Racist or homophobic slurs toward the staff
- Consistently showing up to donate under the influence
- Consistently falling asleep during your donation
- Touching or commenting on staff inappropriately

- Not complying with donor center guidelines (no sunglasses/eye coverings, no eating, drinking, or gum, no videotaping, no photography, etc.)
- A person who weighs under 110 pounds cannot donate
- A donor must be between the ages of 18 and 69.
- A donor must be in good health and not sick during donation.
- Any type of active cancer
- Heart disease
- Certain medications
- If a person has ever tested positive for HIV/Aids
- If a person has ever tested positive for tuberculosis
- And many more

At the beginning of your journey to become a plasma donor, there are certain steps you have to follow that guarantee the safety of the plasma donation. First, you will set up an appointment as a "First Time Donor" and expect it to take anywhere from 2-3 hours. Usually, your appointment will only be about an hour to donate. When you first arrive, you will give the receptionist your two forms of identification and proof of address. Next, they will send you to a phlebotomist to mark your veins as green, yellow, red, or unable to donate. After this, you will fill out a 50-question survey about your medications, conditions, and surgeries that you have had. This is the initial screening for donor eligibility. After this is finished, you will see the on-staff doctor, who will perform a physical evaluation on you. If you pass your physical, the receptionist will poke your finger for a hematocrit, take your weight and temperature, and go through some more screening questions with you. You will then go into the donor queue and wait for your name to be called for donation. Your phlebotomist will walk you through the whole process and set you up for your donation. Next, they will take a small whole blood sample to rule out any diseases and start your donation. If you throw up or pass out, there will be a phlebotomist there to help you and check on you frequently. In the event of syncope or emesis, the donation must be terminated.

Chapter Review

- Hematomas, infiltrations, bruises, and blown veins are a part of the profession of phlebotomy. You will never meet someone who has never once done these things by accident. Sometimes it is unavoidable. When they do occur, calmly explain what happened to your patient and, if needed, get them some ice.
- Clotting and hemolysis happen either by phlebotomist error or just naturally. There are going to be times when you send down a perfectly good sample, and then they mark it as clotted or hemolyzed in the lab. It is up to the laboratory technicians to distinguish what a sufficient sample is. Explain to the patient why the draw is necessary and get another sample. You can always ask for help if you need it. The plasma industry is a great way for a phlebotomist to learn about a lot of different types of veins, skin tones, scar tissue, and people. There can be challenges, just like in any other profession, and things can get uncomfortable.
- Always ask the patient if they are allergic to iodine before applying it since there is such a sensitivity to it. Follow proper guidelines for BAC and other testing that explicitly states the sanitation guidelines.
- Aurora machines require a lot of maintenance and sophistication to work properly. Do not try to use these machines without the proper training. If you have questions, it is better to ask than to break something or mess up someone's donation.
- Hemoglobin and hematocrit are very important in this industry because we are taking more blood away from our patients. Stat labs for hemoglobin blood work guide doctors on whether or not to give a patient a transfusion.

Chapter 6: Legal Side of Phlebotomy

Key terms in this chapter: Contact, Reporting, Power of Attorney, and HIPAA.

Paperwork

Tip #63: Ordering Your Own Lab Work

Although many doctors advise against ordering your own lab work since you most likely will not be able to interpret the results accurately, it is possible. People come in frequently to order pregnancy tests for themselves, hormone levels, etc. This is helpful for couples trying to conceive or for those suffering from lifelong illnesses that they can monitor through blood work. However, most times, insurance will not cover testing that is not ordered by a medical provider. This can mean a test that would be free out of pocket would be charged $150 to your insurance company, or you could pay $30 cash for the same test without having it run through insurance. On top of this, patients are required to sign advanced beneficiary notices for certain testing that state that if insurance does not cover the testing, then it will be billed for a higher amount back to the patient.

Tip #64: Consent to Draw Minors

I work as a phlebotomist in the state of Nebraska. Therefore, a minor for medical services technically constitutes anybody under 19 years of age, rather than the typical age of 18. If I have a patient under 19 who shows up for lab work, it is up to my discretion as to what documentation I am comfortable with. Legally, you simply require consent from their parents or legal guardians; however, this comes in different forms. At certain clinics, they require guardians to be with the minor at all times of the visit so that they can verbally consent or sign paperwork that the minor is not allowed to sign.

At other clinics, the guardians sign waivers stating that they consent to any necessary laboratory testing, medication, exams, etc., that are necessary for their child and that their child consents to. In both of these cases, I have no hesitation in drawing blood from these minors. However, if I had a patient between the ages of 16 and 18 who drove themselves to the lab and didn't have written consent, there would be a gray area. Either I can allow them to call their parents and get consent over the phone, or I can tell them to come back another day. I will never draw a child under the age of 18 if their parents aren't at least consenting over the phone. Sometimes kids try to say, "Oh, well, my parents just told me to come alone." If the parents didn't consent to this testing, they could refuse to pay for the testing and feud with the insurance company over unauthorized use of their insurance. There are tests ranging up to 200 dollars that would be coming out of your company if this were to happen.

On the contrary, working in a hospital has exact consent and paperwork signed for you and the providers upon admission so that you may bypass all of that legality. While you always ask if it's okay.

Tip #65: Advance Beneficiary Notice

There are a few tests that require advanced beneficiary notices to be signed prior to being run due to insurance types, not meeting medical necessity, or the frequency of the testing being done. The most common tests that need an ABN signed are for Hemoglobin A1C and Vitamin D Hydroxy. Hemoglobin A1Cs are covered by insurance once every 90 days, and Vitamin D Hydroxy testing is covered per medical necessity.

Tip #66: Release of Records

Whether your testing is done at a hospital or an outpatient clinic, you have a right to your privacy. Nobody can access the results of your laboratory testing other than the doctor who ordered it until you sign documents stating who you want to have access to it. Unfortunately, this is commonplace in people who see multiple providers and want to send the results to all of them. You even have to sign a release of records to get your results to be sent to yourself.

Personal and Legal Safety

Tip #67: Rights and Responsibilities of a Phlebotomist

My responsibility as a phlebotomist is to do my best to draw the patient's necessary labs without causing any unnecessary pain. If I don't think that I will be able to draw blood or I can't find any suitable veins, I can always call another phlebotomist who I think could possibly be successful. As I mentioned earlier, we have a two-stick rule to prevent us from causing undue pain to the patient. A lot of times, patients won't differentiate your role from the role of nurses and will ask you to do things for them that are not in your scope of practice. This includes asking you to get them a glass of water, reposition them, help them to the bathroom, pour out their urinal, etc. While these all seem like simple tasks, you cannot do any of these as a phlebotomist. If you were to get a glass of water for a patient you didn't know was NPO, their surgery could be postponed. If you reposition them and they have an open skull cap, they could cause brain damage. If you attempt to help them to the bathroom and you don't realize that they are not allowed to get out of the bed, you could cause a traumatic fall. If you empty their urinal and their urine output is strictly monitored, then they could get a decreased dose of antidiuretic that they really need. My go-to answer for any requests is, "I'll let your nurse know; I am not allowed to do that for you."

Tip #68: Obliging Patient Requests/Consent to Draw

When waking patients in the morning, I always start by saying, "Hi! My name is Mackenna, and I am here to grab some blood really quickly." This follows the protocol to introduce yourself, state why you are there and give them a duration of time that you will need. It takes me around four minutes to scan the patient's wristband, confirm their name and birthday, prepare my equipment, and draw their blood. If a patient asks you to come back later, it is necessary to ask the patient's nurse before exiting the room. If a patient is on heparin, they are on a strict schedule of blood draws to check their clotting time. In these cases, the nurse will talk to the patient about how important it is for the blood to be drawn on schedule. If the patient still refuses, the nurse typically will tell the patient's medical team and tell you to try again in an hour. This is possible only if a patient is mentally competent. If a patient is suicidal, demented, or somehow not able to make decisions for themselves, the nurses will hold down the patient while you are drawing their blood since you have consent from the patient's power of attorney. You do not need the patient's direct consent in these situations.

Tip #69: How to Handle Combative Patients

Combative patients are all special in their own way. Before judging them, you need to understand that they have failing organs, mental problems, drug abuse, brain trauma, etc. All these things affect a person's brain and can make them act like someone they are not. Other times there are patients who have dementia or those that are just sick and tired of getting blood drawn and have been in the hospital for months. There are multiple different types of restraints for patients that range from just having their hands padded to being in four-point restraints with a spit hood on. Patients who are intubated and not completely paralyzed must have their hands restrained so they don't attempt to pull out their breathing tube. In other situations, dementia patients will need to be restrained to prevent them from pulling out their IVs.

Tip #70: How to Handle Verbal and Physical Assault

Coming at people with needles at three o'clock in the morning comes with being physically and verbally assaulted. This can range from profanities to slander and racial slurs. If you are being verbally attacked by a patient who is mentally coherent, tell them that they have the right to refuse blood work, and if they continue to harass you, then you will leave. Likewise, if the patient starts to make threats such as "I'm going to kill you," "I'm going to hit you," or anything else, you should immediately leave the room. If you fear for your safety being close to the patient, you may leave your supplies on the bed until you can get a nurse to accompany you to get your equipment. We receive specific training on personal defense against violent patients as hospital staff. It is a felony in the state of Nebraska to assault a certified medical professional in the pursuit of performing their job. It is not uncommon for a patient to attempt to hit, bite, scratch, kick, and spit on medical professionals if they are not in their right mind. The second someone touches you in a way that is inappropriate or threatening, you back away from the patient. If you cannot put distance between yourself and the patient, you start screaming. If you are fearing for your life or fighting off a patient, you are advised on ways to push them off and protect yourself. The problem that arises from pushing off a patient who is trying to attack you is the fact that patients on blood thinners bruise extremely easily. Simply holding their arm down from hitting you can leave a huge bruise. So, while you should always protect yourself, have a nurse accompany you if you are uncomfortable around a certain patient or if other coworkers have warned you.

Chapter Review

- Ordering your own lab work is increasingly more popular among people who want to pay cash and interpret their own results.
- Drawing minors in an outpatient setting requires parent consent, either written or in person. In some instances,

verbal consent is appropriate if the phlebotomist is comfortable with accepting it as consent.

- Drawing minors in the hospital does not require parental consent directly to the phlebotomist because the parents or guardians have already signed hospital consent forms that cover any necessary care.
- Obliging patient requests only in the scope of your practice is the safest way to follow the rules and stay within good standing with the nurses.

Follow hospital procedures when it comes to combative patients and verbally abusive patients. Most rooms will have a warning on the door to contact the nurse and not enter the room alone. In extreme cases, call security if you don't believe the staff can handle the patient alone.

About the Author

MacKenna Balsewicz is a 20-year-old mother of one who has spent the last three years working as a phlebotomist at different professional facilities. She started her training at Biomat Plasma Center, where she gained the confidence and skill to draw blood and care for donors. After working at Biomat for 12 months, she transferred to Bryan Hospital to work in the laboratory department. She has fallen in love with performing phlebotomy in the hospital setting and now works at Nebraska Medicine, where she draws upwards of 60 people daily. Along with being a phlebotomist, she will be graduating from the University of Nebraska Lincoln in May of 2023 with her bachelor's degree in Psychology.

HowExpert publishes how to guides by everyday experts. Visit HowExpert.com to learn more.

Recommended Resources

- HowExpert.com – How To Guides by Everyday Experts.
- HowExpert.com/free – Free HowExpert Email Newsletter.
- HowExpert.com/books – HowExpert Books
- HowExpert.com/courses – HowExpert Courses
- HowExpert.com/clothing – HowExpert Clothing
- HowExpert.com/membership – HowExpert Membership Site
- HowExpert.com/affiliates – HowExpert Affiliate Program
- HowExpert.com/jobs – HowExpert Jobs
- HowExpert.com/writers – Write About Your #1 Passion/Knowledge/Expertise & Become a HowExpert Author.
- HowExpert.com/resources – Additional HowExpert Recommended Resources
- YouTube.com/HowExpert – Subscribe to HowExpert YouTube.
- Instagram.com/HowExpert – Follow HowExpert on Instagram.
- Facebook.com/HowExpert – Follow HowExpert on Facebook.
- TikTok.com/@HowExpert – Follow HowExpert on TikTok.

CPSIA information can be obtained
at www.ICGtesting.com
Printed in the USA
LVHW111404190822
726376LV00003B/20